TALES FROM THE CUT

TALES FROM THE CUT

TRUE STORIES ABOUT THE U.S. ARMY'S COMBAT LAND CLEARING ENGINEERS IN VIETNAM

Presented by
Terry T. Brown

ABOOKS

Alive Book Publishing

Tales from The Cut
True Stories About U.S. Army Combat
Land Clearing Engineers in Vietnam
Copyright © 2022 by Terry T. Brown

Additional copies may be ordered from the publisher for
educational, business, promotional or premium use.
For information, contact ALIVE Book Publishing at:
alivebookpublishing.com

Book Interior and Cover Design by Alex P. Johnson
Cover Photo Courtesy U.S. Army Corps of Engineers

ISBN 13
978-1-63132-186-3

Library of Congress Control Number: 2022921627
Library of Congress Cataloging-in-Publication Data
is available upon request.

First Edition

Published in the United States of America by ALIVE Book Publishing
an imprint of Advanced Publishing LLC, Alamo, California, USA
alivebookpublishing.com

PRINTED IN THE UNITED STATES OF AMERICA

10 9 8 7 6 5 4 3 2 1

Contents

The Secret

The secret of it all, is to write in the gush, the throb, the flood of the moment – to put things down without deliberation – without worrying about their style – without waiting for a fit time or place. I always worked that way. I took the first scrap of paper, the first doorstep, the first desk, and wrote – wrote, wrote...By writing at the instant, the very heartbeat of life is caught.

~Walt Whitman

Acknowledgements

I wish to thank all those whose generous contribution to this book had helped in shaping its content, while it also gave me pause to appreciate the other writer's styles and ways of conveying their points of view, with regard to their own life experiences as land clearing engineers in Vietnam. Their shared remembrances had helped to bring back many old memories from a bygone era, while working in a war zone far away from home, where most of them had simply made the best of their situation, despite not wanting to be there.

Special thanks and recognition also goes out to the Vietnam Land Clearers Association, whose overall members had helped in forming the ideas behind the collective concept of this book.

But mostly, in helping to bring many of these short stories to the pages of this book, I would like to single out and thank fellow land clearer Tom Randle Jr of Clayton, Georgia, who had originally suggested the multi-story format involving writings from various authors. He also wrote the Forward and provided his own short story as well, while even getting some of the other participating writers to submit their own stories through his Vietnam Land Clearers' Facebook page. Without his contributing efforts along those lines this book most likely would not have been possible.

When putting it all together on the pages, some of the featured pictures and images shown throughout this book were gleaned from stock public domain photos that were found on the internet, while most of the others came from my own individual collection and those contributed by others.

Also, I give thanks to my good friend Thea Fey for her photographic knowledge and assistance, in helping to add to things.

Additionally, I wish to give credit to the late Army engineer historian, Major General Robert R. Ploger, who passed away in September of 2002, for key historical information about the earlier formation of Land Clearing in Vietnam, which I learned when reading his book: *Vietnam Studies: U.S. Army Engineers, 1965 – 1970.*

Dedication

This book is honorably dedicated to all of the men who had participated with Land Clearing operations in South Vietnam. No matter their role, they all served as team members in their assigned tasks, to keep the operations flowing and moving forward. Their grit and determination in completing their missions while faced with adverse conditions and enemy opposition was the key to achieving the overall success from their jungle cutting excursions, which ultimately resulted in greater security and control for the U.S. and allied forces. But perhaps most notably, many lives had also been saved in the process, from the constant threat of roadside ambushes where the Viet Cong guerrillas had been routinely using the jungle as effective cover for their signature 'hit and run' nightmare tactics of insurgent warfare. However, with the significant removal of the thick jungle growth all along these highways having created wider open areas on both sides of the roads for greater fields of view, it then allowed military convoys and civilian traffic to safely pass and go on through to their destinations without the looming threat of being attacked along the way. As a major breakthrough during the war, this was an enormous development that took shape to effectively counter and curtail the Viet Cong's formerly unchallenged acts of forward aggression.

Prior to the advent of the Rome Plow tractor in Vietnam, many South Vietnamese and U.S. military convoys on the move had been mercilessly attacked while receiving small arms fire and rocket propelled grenades from along the jungle-covered edges or shoulders of the various regional two-lane roadways. The Viet Cong had simply been lying in wait like hungry predators, hiding behind their naturally growing cover of trees and broad leaved tropical shrubs, before unleashing their barrage of terror and destruction that nearly always resulted in numerous casualties of dead and wounded soldiers and South Vietnamese civilians. As this grim activity was trending and growing as a hazard to be expected on occasion along the many roadways where convoys and other vehicles had created regular flows of traffic, nobody seemed to have an immediate answer to effectively quell this alarming problem.

But with the rapid development of the amazing jungle-cutting Rome Plow tractors during the height of the war, several company-size Army engineer units had been formed in the I Corps, II Corps, and III Corps tactical zones of South Vietnam to help counter these deadly guerrilla tactics of the Viet Cong and NVA insurgents. As a result, much had been accomplished from the Rome Plow's tactical disbursements into these targeted areas of operation, and much of the intended carnage as a result had been stopped or diverted.

In addition to all whom this book is dedicated to, it also serves to honor the many men who were wounded in action while perfoming their duties as land clearers. But, more notably, it serves to honor the memory of all those men who were killed in action (KIAs); having lost their lives while working at this risky endeavor called Land Clearing. Some were killed in various ways by the Viet Cong and NVA forces, by way of reactionary tactics of retaliation for attacking and removing their natural base of concealment, while some others had died as a result of tragic accidents that occurred from time to time, due to various circumstances and situations. But their loss, no matter the cause nor the circumstance, was everyone's loss, and they shall not be forgotten.

This granite stone memorial, which stands on the grounds of the Rome Plow Company in Cedartown, Georgia, was dedicated in the Summer of 2012 to honor all who had served in South Vietnam as U.S. Army Land Clearing engineers; with special recognition to those named within who forfeited their lives during the course of working to save the lives of others, while improving on the overall security within the country. The commemorative monolith serves to show that their ultimate sacrifice does not go unnoticed.

Foreword

Over the years, historians have poured over the Vietnam War in excruciating detail. But you may not know that almost none of them had served in the armed forces in Vietnam. Therein lies the rub.

In "Tales from the Cut," author Terry T. Brown, who served in one of the many land clearing companies featured in the book, and had previously published *"Clearing Vietnam: Anatomy of a U.S. Army Land Clearing Team,"* 2007, ISBN 0-7414-3974-3, knows what the men of the "Rome Plow" units had lived through. However, because of the serious nature of this involvement, approximately fifty men died in action as a result of their own participation with land clearing operations in Vietnam.

The difficult and dangerous job of clearing away the jungle so that the People's Army of North Vietnam (NVA) could not move supplies and troops undetected was an insane idea fomented by military intelligence; an oxymoron if ever there was.

Often called "Viet Cong," "VC," or simply "Charlie," the enemy was Soviet-backed, along with support from Communist China and other Communist-connected movements in the region. U.S. troops, who were directly supporting the South Vietnam government were joined in that role by other allies, including Australia, New Zealand, South Korea, and Thailand. The men of the various Rome Plow companies were alternately defended on each operation by a company of mobile troops, in the form of

Aussies, Thai Rangers, or Korean soldiers, as well as their own U.S. contingent of mechanized armored cavalry soldiers.

A typical Rome Plow company was comprised of 100 men with 30 Caterpillar D7-E tractors; 28 of which were converted into Rome Plows while the remaining two were kept as Bull Blade dozers. What made them Rome Plows were the attachable KG blade and mounted cab that provided some measure of protection to the operators.

These unique Rome Plow accessories were built in Cedartown, Georgia, by a company that originally began in Rome, Georgia. You can still find a KG blade from the 1960's on sale for about $2,000. The company itself, still exists to this day in Cedartown, dealing mostly in various types of tilling equipment for farm tractors.

Over fifty years have passed since land clearing and the war ended in Vietnam. The many thousands of acres destroyed back then have since re-grown to a large extent, to re-form with the areas of jungle that hadn't been touched. The new growth now effectively covers the scars that were left on the landscape, while the wounds of the men who performed one of the hardest, hottest, most dangerous jobs have not healed entirely.

Through bi-annual reunions, all of the men still living who served in any land clearing team/unit/company are regularly invited to attend and be part of a celebration of their own legacy, and to pay tribute by honoring their fallen members, while the gatherings also serve as a time for renewal from old psychological wounds. Their related stories are commonly shared with their buddies, and with other former land clearers with whom they didn't know, as a way to heal, bond and share. Tears are shed, while former battle buddies are suddenly reunited after not seeing each other for decades.

This book is a compilation of the stories some of them have shared. Many others are still unable to write their own story. But hopefully this book will serve to comfort them, along with their families who may still not know exactly what they experienced, given that some of these men are not willing to even discuss it.

Tom Randle
60th Engineer Co (LC) "Jungle Eaters" - Vietnam
1969 – 1970

Author of "Dad, What Did You Do in Vietnam," 2020, ISBN 9798692034120, available on Amazon.

Prologue

It gives me a great deal of pleasure to be able to present this unique conglomeration of short stories and related history from a time when all of the writers featured here were so young and directly involved with their own personal experiences and daily encounters related to Land Clearing operations in Vietnam. Given that everyone's remembrances from those days when serving within their respective land clearing unit were somewhat different, each of these men's stories actually tie into the main theme from their own job-related viewpoint. Their combined recollections from an earlier time, make it abundantly clear that there were various connecting elements and aspects involved with the assembly, logistics, and overall application of land clearing operations, as this newly developed form of tactical engineer support was found to be multi-faceted but well-coordinated in its overall methods of implementation.

Interestingly, as land clearing combat engineers, these unique units as defined by the Army were given a more specific designation with their type of deployment, being referred to as Tactical Land Clearing Engineers, which had in later years been noted as a new historic achievement in warfare, given the fact that throughout the history of the U.S. Army Corps of Engineers, none of its represented units in combat had ever been specifically named or designated as a tactical force, while heavy construction type equipment in any form, had also never been used previously in a tactical sort of way against enemy forces.

But, in relating the various recalled experiences that these short story writers touch on in this book, the majority of the collection were found to have been written in more recent times, after around 40 to 50 years or so removed from these men's tours in Vietnam; although one of them in particular had actually been scribed while the man was still serving as a medic in his assigned land clearing unit, and another was written as a timeline of events conveyed from within old letters that were sent home by one the equipment mechanics during his 12 month tour. Given that so much time had passed before these writings were finally put forth, they were all still found to be honest accountings from the men who were there, as remembered from their time in-country, in re-telling their stories about some of the more unusual events and encounters they had 'eyes-on' and first-hand knowledge of.

While I am just one of the contributing authors for this book of stories, I am also actually noted on the cover and the inside introductory page as simply being the 'presenter' for all of the other authors here, whose own important part in this joint writing effort is one of equal value, in reflecting on the different aspects involved with their various haunting remembrances about their own encounters with land clearing operations from a time so very long ago, in a far off unforgotten land.

Interestingly, the public media's rather limited telling of the story of Land Clearing operations in Vietnam, from its historic perspective, has never really gotten all that much coverage or notice over the years; although it is truly a story worth noting in its entirety, in bringing further recognition of its overall importance to the forefront.

Given the many positive benefits that were achieved through the Rome Plow's initial deployment as a 'great experiment' in tactical warfare during the height of the war, it is important to point out that a quite notable improvement in the country's overall security was eventually realized. It all came of age due to the immediate need to develop a plan to help counter the Viet Cong and NVA force's out-of-control insurgency and the mass carnage that came along with it. This plan was in direct response to a dire situation where enemy forces, while finding sanctuary within the protective confines of the jungle, were conveniently using the available heavy cover to their full advantage, as a natural form of concealment for their highly destructive covert activities.

For that particular purpose, while the clearing process over time had fit the bill perfectly in solving that major problem in Vietnam, it is my belief that land clearing will likely never again be needed in a wartime scenario. As it is recognized today by historians, I believe that tactical land clearing will only be seen in history as an extreme measure of resolve that was utilized quite successfully in the Vietnam war to help get a better handle on the seemingly uncontrolable guerrilla warfare practiced by the Viet Cong and NVA soldiers, with their relentless tactics of insurgency that posed a serious threat to security within that country. Moreover, in achieving its targeted goal of greatly improving on the country's overall level of security throughout its four military tactical regions, the Rome Plow had also managed to save countless lives as a direct result of the clearing process, as it was applied to roadways.

But, with this collective offering of various short stories put forth here, more interesting aspects of the unusual or unconventional story of Land Clearing in Vietnam are revealed, in the form of human-interest type remembrances that convey more about some of the grim realities of war, along with certain hardships involved, and the engineer soldier's simple yet arduous life in the field. Plus, they even touch on some of the little-known absurdities that were occasionally encountered, which tend to just make us all chuckle a bit.

Among the many viewpoints given on the war in Vietnam, some observers have suggested that if Land Clearing had actually begun only a year or two earlier than it did, they believe that the Rome Plow would have more dramatically altered the landscape in such a way, to where enemy supply lines, which had been flowing over the Ho Chi Minh Trail and along other key routes, would have likely been disrupted and stymied for the most part. The thinking here suggests that NVA forces and Viet Cong guerrillas might have then been forced to withdraw back to the north or into Cambodia with the realized loss of their all-important sancuaries of cover; to perhaps at least possibly bring about the consideration of an eventual settlement in the form of an Armistice, much like what had previously occurred in 1953 with North and South Korea.

But you know what they say about hindsight...

Terry T. Brown
86th LCT & 501st LCC, Vietnam
1968 – 1969

The U.S. Army Corps of Engineers

Courtesy of www.usace.army.mil

George Washington appointed the first engineer officers of the Army on June 16, 1775, during the American Revolution, and engineers have served in combat in all subsequent American wars. The Army established the Corps of Engineers as a separate, permanent branch on March 16, 1802, and gave the engineers responsibility for founding and operating the U.S. Military Academy at West Point.

Since then, the U.S. Army Corps of Engineers has responded to changing defense requirements and played an integral part in the development of the country. Throughout the 19th century, the Corps built coastal fortifications, surveyed roads and canals, eliminated navigational hazards, explored and mapped the Western frontier, and constructed buildings and monuments in the Nation's capital.

From the beginning, many politicians wanted the Corps to contribute to both military construction and works "of a civil nature." Throughout the 19th century, the Corps supervised the construction of coastal fortifications and mapped much of the American West with the Corps of Topographical Engineers, which enjoyed a separate existence for 25 years (1838-1863). The Corps of Engineers also constructed lighthouses, helped develop jetties and piers for harbors, and carefully mapped the navigation channels.

In the 20th century, the Corps became the lead federal flood control agency and significantly expanded its civil works activities, becoming among other things a major provider of hydroelectric energy and the country's leading provider of recreation. Its role in responding to natural disasters also grew dramatically.

Assigned the military construction mission in 1941, the Corps built facilities at home and abroad to support the U.S. Army and Air Force. During the Cold War, Army engineers managed construction programs for America's allies, including a massive effort in Saudi Arabia. In addition, the Corps of Engineers also completed large construction programs for federal agencies such as NASA and the postal service.. The Corps also maintains a rigorous research and development program in support of its water resources, construction, and military activities.

In the late 1960s, the Corps became a leading environmental preservation and restoration agency. It now carries out natural and cultural resource management programs at its water resources projects and regulates activities in the Nation's wetlands. In addition, the Corps assists the military services in environmental management and restoration at former and current military installations.

When the Cold War ended, the Corps was poised to support the Army and the Nation in the new era. Army engineers supported 9/11 recovery efforts and currently play an important international role in the rapidly evolving Global War on Terrorism, including reconstruction in Iraq and Afghanistan. The U.S. Army Corps of Engineers stands ready to support the country's military and water resources needs in the 21st century as it has done during its more than two centuries of service.

Introduction

The History of
Land Clearing in South Vietnam

What turned out to be probably the most important achievement of the U.S. Army Corps of Engineers in Vietnam, had to do with their practical application of a workable solution to a serious ongoing security problem. By developing unique jungle cutting tractors for deployment into particular troublesome areas where the Viet Cong had been using the natural foliage of the land to their advantage, the Army had responded by coming up with a viable means of neutralizing that natural advantage. The impressive method of applying acquired land clearing tactics and techniques with the use of specially equipped crawler tractors during the height of the War, to effectively cut down and eliminate thick tropical jungle growth in order to gain better access and visibility, had served as one of the most effective tactical moves ever applied in a war zone.

The expected arrival of these efficient jungle cutting tractors was seen by many early-on, as a promising, if not vital means of improving the overall security throughout the four tactical zones of South Vietnam. By design, they were unleashed to significantly change the overall make-up of the landscape in many key areas where the Viet Cong and NVA forces had formerly established their routes of infiltration and underground bases of operation.

As this newly hatched innovation had naturally grown and evolved from the early deployment of land clearing units, the Army engineers involved with it had become more widely known for their 'no nonsense' approach toward eliminating the Viet Cong's jungle-covered sanctuaries by penetrating areas where enemy strongholds had previously controlled the flow of food and munitions for the enemy combatants. Upon entering these known areas where enemy activity was present, these engineers boldly invaded and destroyed many of their labyrinth-like systems of underground tunnels that were found to contain stored caches of rice and various weapons and ammunition. These operational deployments had also served to open up key roadways where the constant threat of ambushes had previously been quite prevalent; to then allow for traffic to flow freely again, unencumbered by that previous threat, thanks to the overall efforts of these highly motivated and determined combat engineers.

Oftentimes, when entering known areas of enemy activity, these engineer soldiers and their well-maintained Caterpillar D7E tractors called Rome Plows, which were outfitted with specially designed cutting blades and steel reinforced cabs, had commonly formed the vanguard of assault forces when attacking fortified enemy positions. They occasionally served as the operation's 'tip of the spear' when used as an effective tactical force inside the jungle, whenever the enemy's concealed bases of operation were suddenly detected. Otherwise, during normal cuts, the plows were still the first to enter the jungle, while the mechanized security elements, consisting of tanks and Armored Personnel Carriers, could only observe the process while keeping close enough to the tractors to provide assistance and cover fire if needed, in the event of an organized enemy attack or an isolated incident.

As the process evolved, these groups of somewhat rag-tag engineer soldiers had developed a certain amount of pride in the importance, difficulty, and resourcefulness associated with their job placement as land clearers; and while matters of their appearance had largely taken a back seat to the job at hand, their morale and spirit, and overall level of confidence displayed on a daily basis, while working under adverse conditions, tended to make up for their apparent lack of good grooming. But with their overall dedication to the land clearing mission as combat engineers, their notably longer hair and unshaven faces, while living out in the jungle for 45 days at a stretch without any barbers present, had become much less of an important factor to their unit leaders.

As the eventful story of Land Clearing in Vietnam had unfolded, General William Westmoreland, in 1965, had assigned his staff members at * MACV (Military Assistance Command Vietnam) in Saigon with the task of seeing what it might take to come up with a possible solution to the kinds of serious out-of-control security problems encountered daily throughout the four militarized regions of the country. Their inquiring efforts, in arriving at a solution, had decidedly been focused on finding a workable method that would effectively remove the jungle in many of the trouble-spot areas, in order to take away the Viet Cong's free and easy use of it as tactical cover.

In the initial experimental stage of this inquiry, several different unique types of machinery had been proposed for consideration, and were sent to a couple of selected engineer units near Saigon for staging and thorough testing and evaluation. One of these premeire land clearing testing units was the 557th Engineer Company (LE). Among the narrowed-down equipment candidates for possible consideration were a 100-ton tracked tanklike vehicle, plus the giant 3-wheeled Le Tourneau tree-crusher, and a Rome Plow attachable cutting blade for military tractors.

The <u>Military Assistance Command, Vietnam – Studies and Observation Group</u>, otherwise known as MACV, was a highly classified special operations unit, which had conducted covert unconventional warfare operations during the Vietnam war, involving strategic reconnaissance, covert action, and psychological warfare.

Le Tourneau Tree Crusher

Allis Chalmers HD-16 Tractor with Rome Plow blade & cab

M548 Maintenance / Cargo Track Vehicle

Caterpillar D7E Tractor with Rome Plow blade & cab

As it turned out, from all of the various proposed pieces of equipment tested to take on the difficult task at hand during land clearing's formative period of development, it was the Caterpillar D7E crawler tractor that emerged as the 'hands down' winner; while smartly equipped with a specially designed cutting blade and a steel-reinforced cab, to transform it from a basic bulldozer into what was then referred to as a ' Rome Plow.' With the addition of mine guards, heavy steel engine guards, thick perforated steel plates to protect the radiator, and steel protective belly pans covering the underside of the engine and transmission, it was then made ready for full deployment to take on the Army's intended objective.

The uniquely designed blade and cab were both manufactured and distributed to South Vietnam by the Rome Plow Company of Cedartown, Georgia. Over the years, this company in northwest Georgia was largely known as a farm implement type manufacturer and distributor, having been established in 1934, while mainly specializing in tillage type attachments for farm tractors. The unique K/G blade had actually been designed and developed by its inventor, Ernest Kissner of Lottie, Louisiana, during the early 1950's. It was subsequently acquired by the Rome Plow Company in 1957.

This special re-equipped Caterpillar tractor with its 4-cylinder turbo charged diesel engine and its 3-speed forward and 3-speed reverse automatic shift transmission, along with the addition of a Rome Plow cutting blade and steel reinforced tree cab, was found to be the most practical way of accomplishing the task, in addressing the targeted objective. It was also found to be more easily transportable by flat-bed trailer to areas all around the country.

Essentially, this unusual tractor assembly was chosen as the most effective method overall, in performing at a high rate of production, toward reducing and eliminating many thousands of acres of high-canopied tropical jungle in the shortest possible amount of time. But the plow's main feature, serving as the perfect tool for cutting down heavy foliage and trees, was the imposing 30 degree canted and curved blade, with its routinely sharpened leading edge, stinger, and mounted brush guards all combining to highlight its unique and practical design. In application, this unusual angled cutting blade with its top mounted brush guards, effectively guided the cut debris from the knife-like leading edge, to conveniently push it all aside to the right as the tractor progressed. As it moved along and sliced through the thick brush and smaller trees, the tractor would continue to crawl forward against the heavy growth with relative ease in targeting either roadside areas to eliminate the cover there, or some of the key places where the Viet Cong had been more inclined to take up refuge and establish their hidden bases of operation.

During this initial testing process in 1966, as these various pieces of equipment were being evaluated, the Rome Plow attachments had also been applied to the Allis Chalmers HD-16 tractor, which was very close in size with the Cat D7E, and had seemingly performed just as well. The HD-16 was also fully hydraulic and easily driven by way of an automatic transmission. In its own trials, it was found to have held up quite well against the challenges within the cut, while a few of these similarly designed AC tractors had actually been retained and used in some situations in Vietnam as Rome Plows. Although, it is suspected that since Caterpillar was such a widely recognized international company with a larger assembly line and manufacturer base of support, that there may have been some natural bias with the Department of the Army in giving the Cat D7E the nod to become the featured track vehicle-of-choice to wear the Rome K/G blade and cab, in fully forming the iron icon that ultimately became synonymous with land clearing in Vietnam.

This rather large and canted Rome Plow blade, with its featured leading edge, was specifically designed in another thoughtful way, to allow for foliage to be cut no lower than 6 inches from the ground. By effectively shearing off the vegetation at a height where the root structure would remain fully intact, it effectively prevented soil erosion, and even allowed for future regrowth. The dozer's engineer operators, in the course of their daily maintenance tasks, would additionally take time to routinely apply a nearly razor-sharp edge to the beveled cutting area of the tractor's protruding blade with the use of a pneumatic grinder that was powered by a diesel air compressor. At the leading corner of the blade, an extended steel wedge called a 'Stinger', jutted out by about a foot or 0.3 meters to serve as the blade's pointed tool for splitting and felling large trees that were regularly encountered. In application, the operator would attack a tree by making a stabbing pass at its trunk, while maneuvering and angling the tractor with each pass to make successive stabbings, in chipping away at it by carving out chunks of wood until the trunk would eventually be reduced to where it would begin to splinter and crack, and the tree would then fall to the floor of the jungle.

After developing more effective methods of utilizing the Rome Plow's unique capabilities during 1966, three land clearing platoons had arrived in South Vietnam from Fort Lewis, Washington in the Spring of 1967, with two of them setting up their bases of operations within the III Corps Tactical Zone. These three were the very first units that were formed, to begin taking on the organized task of clearing targeted areas of jungle where the Viet Cong were known to be present. One of these platoons had been assigned to the 86th Engineer Battalion in Bearcat Basecamp (*southeast of Saigon*), to serve as a special detachment, while the other land clearing platoon had joined with the 168th Engineer Battalion (*located north of Saigon*), in Di An, as both of these newly arrived units had thereby become an important addition to the 20th Engineer Brigade. They were known as the 86th and 27th Land Clearing Platoons, respectively. The third unit, numerically known as the 35th Land Clearing Platoon, was sent north from there to take up residency within the II Corps Tactical zone of operations in the central highland region, serving under the 18th Engineer Brigade.

By the Summer of 1967, all three of these platoons were fully operational, after each had been equipped with 30 Caterpillar D7E tractors, along with Rome Plow kits that had to be assembled and installed. With a fresh coat of Army olive drab paint to freshen their outward appearance and help keep their visibility somewhat neutral against the backdrop of the jungle; and with large identifying white numbers also applied to each one, in order to distinguish them from a distance, the tractors were finally ready for their fully organized entry into the cut. Various nicknames were also applied to the sides and rear of the cabs, as the operators were given clearance to do so, within reason and good taste.

With further regard to all three of these new land clearing units, the 'platoon' aspect of their unit identity had only lasted for several months throughout 1967, as that particular designation had changed in early 1968 to where they all had then come to be known as Land Clearing Teams. At that stage of development, each of these Teams had an overall make-up of 64 men, which seemed rather meager for manning the 30 Caterpillar tractors and other related equipment; plus, also in having to provide a large enough contingent of maintenance personnel to tackle all of the needed repairs during an operation, while serving the needs of two tractor platoons, each consisting of 14 plows and 1 bull blade dozer. *However, in time that number would increase to 100 men, with 3 plow platoons featuring 9 plows and 1 bull blade dozer per platoon.*

In practical military application, land clearing operations had employed three basic types of cuts with the use of this new Rome Plow tractor:

(1) The <u>Area Cut</u> was developed to open up vast areas of landscape, in providing an Infantry Division within their area of operation with more open access and a broader line-of-sight across the wide lanes of cleared landscape, to help with their overall security concerns.

(2) <u>Road cuts</u> were quite common and very much needed in many areas where South Vietnamese and U.S. convoys traveled through on a regular basis. These cuts had created an open landscape of 100 meters or more on both sides of the roadways to help keep Viet Cong and NVA ambushes in check.

(3) <u>Tactical cuts</u> were occasionally used, with several of the plows being lined up side-by-side, before crawling directly in through the jungle in unison with blades raised,

while the mechanized security unit's tanks and APC's trailed just behind. This practice was sometimes utilized when known enemy bases or encampments were detected nearby within the cut, as it forced the enemy to flee, for the most part, while their underground tunnels could then be searched for their supplies before blowing them up with C-4 plastic explosives.

A very important, if not critical part of most land clearing operations in Vietnam had to do with deploying the Rome Plows on Road Cuts, which had served to greatly improve upon the security along key roadways where military supplies and equipment had regularly been transported by convoys traveling through to their destinations. Vietnamese civilian traffic had also flowed daily over the asphalt covered roads, as numerous Lambretta tricycle-type motorized carts would often be seen moving fruits and vegetables to market, along with whatever else they could carry at their slower pace of travel.

But the unforeseen problem for the aforementioned travelers had to do with the fact that these two-lane highways regularly ran through areas of thick jungle growth that came right down to the edges of the roads. So, for all who traveled along these winding tree-lined ribbons of jungle enshrouded blacktop, many were periodically subjected to surprise attacks by the Viet Cong, as the Communist guerrillas were simply using the jungle overgrowth to their advantage, by effectively shielding themselves behind the standing cover along the roadside to become somewhat invisible to passing motorists until the opportune time was right for them to step out and make their appearance known.

With this seemingly unstoppable guerilla type tactic of

warfare being utilized quite regularly by the Viet Cong to their full advantage along these somewhat busy roadways, many of the military convoys and civilian vehicles attempting to travel on through, had been routinely attacked with 'small arms' AK-47 rifle fire and rocket propelled grenades. The perpetrators were always able to make their getaway cleanly and quickly, back in through the thick, tropical, high-canopied forest which had also served as their sanctuary and base of operations, while often having left numerous casualties in their wake. Over time, the casualties mounted in the form of dead and wounded, along with multiple vehicle and equipment damages which had often resulted in partial or complete destruction to their payloads. This openly rampant and out of control activity, at some point had signaled to MACV in Saigon that something needed to be done to effectively curb this insane practice and keep it from happening.

As it turned out, the answer soon came, like the Cavalry coming to the rescue, in the form of the Rome Plow tractor. By effectively cutting the jungle back along both sides of these roads to one hundred meters or more with the use of these heavy tractors, it effectively curtailed the VC's hit and run tactics of warfare, as they soon found that they were no longer able to stage their formerly undetectable roadside ambushes without the natural protective cover in place.

Another notable fringe benefit realized in the aftermath of this jungle clearing process, had to do with the many open/exposed areas where farmers had soon discovered the soil to be rich and fertile for prime cultivation after removing the downed brush and tree roots, as newly productive farmlands had suddenly been created where these areas of thick tropical jungle had once stood. As a result of new crop harvests, an increase in local commerce soon followed, to naturally bring about the sudden rise of new villages within many of these formerly remote, uninhabited areas.

But, as the need for land clearing grew, with the prospect of added security being developed in this way throughout other areas of the country, made possible by the invaluable use of the Rome Plow tractor, the need for additional equipment and more land clearing units had also grown exponentially. At the time, many of the various infantry divisions in their own respective areas of operation were becoming tired of having to wait in line for their turn with the few existing land clearing units available to them, while casualties from ambushes and firefights in their regional areas were steadily on the rise.

So, in December of 1968, the two land clearing teams of the 20th Engineer Brigade, after joining together briefly with the 168th Engineer Battalion in Di An, had then moved their base of operation to Long Binh Post, to take up with the 62nd Engineer Battalion after their lettered construction companies were inactivated. With this newly redirected Engineer Battalion having switched its designation from construction to land clearing, three new Rome Plow companies were then formed from the previous assemblage of the two Teams of the 86th and 27th. As this realignment came about, the 501st, the 60th, and the 984th Land Clearing companies had then emerged to become fully supported Rome Plow units within an unprecedented land clearing battalion, each now containing a working force of 100 men. The newly aligned battalion was also formed with additional maintenance facillities to serve each of these three plow companies, in supporting them with a larger assortment of available parts and attachments, along with a 3rd shop maintenance facillity where complete tear-downs and overhauls on these tractors could then be more easily accomplished, before trucking them back out to rejoin with the operation and the other plows in the cut.

In addition to the new land clearing battalion at Long Binh, just one month later in January of 1969, three more land clearing companies in the two northern tactical zones were created, as the 59th, the 538th, and the 687th Land Clearing companies had been established as new members of the 18th Engineer Brigade. Among those, the 538th was actually transformed from the original 35th Land Clearing Team, to then become a newly lettered LC company within the II Corps or Central Highland region of the country. That brought the number to six overall, until the 501st was later deactivated under the terms of the ordered phase-down in April of 1970.

Given land clearing's early positive results, with its steady rise in popularity becoming more apparent throughout the country, the utilization of the Rome Plow tractor with its newly realized capabilities had come to be seen as more of an essential tool that everyone wanted, in serving their own immediate needs toward attaining and maintaining their own higher levels of security.

As things regarding these tractors had developed further during 1968 and 1969, with Rome Plow kits and additional Caterpillar tractors in higher demand, many more had been ordered and supplied to other engineer units like the 591st and 595th Light Equipment companies, to support their own adopted involvement with land clearing activities in their given operational areas. In time, because of this customized dozer's overall capability and what it meant security-wise, nearly all of the engineer battalions in South Vietnam had at least one or two Rome Plows at their disposal to serve their immediate needs in their own respective areas of operation.

While all of these additional land clearing efforts were building, it wasn't at all uncommon to find even artillery fire-support bases having at least one or two Rome Plows available to them as well, in helping to increase the outer perimeters around their somewhat small and remote fire bases. As needed, they would also be used to occasionally carve out and create landing zones for helicopters to safely touch down and take off from.

The overall topography within the landscape of the III Corps Tactical zone had mostly featured large, reasonably level tracts of tree-lined tropical forests that were, in certain areas, also occupied by substantial numbers of enemy units. Because of their unwelcome and disruptive presence, these particularly troublesome areas of jungle-covered landscape were then found to be in serious need of interdiction, where Rome Plow units were often called upon to apply their skills while taking up the task.

In setting many of the initial guidelines, a great deal was learned from the originally deployed land clearing platoons of 1967. As it pertained to large scale operations, certain techniques had been developed and perfected at that time, to effectively solve particular problems with regard to vital communication between both the land clearers and the mechanized security force, along with that of the lead plow on the cut. This was especially important when the security elements were engaged in a firefight with the enemy. Other particular techniques were additionally developed by the plow operators themselves, from trial-and-error involvements with their tractors on a daily basis, as well as by some of the mechanics when making repairs in the cut. These had all been recognized and passed on for future operators and mechanics to take note of.

The extreme heat, the dust (*or mud during the monsoon season*), large falling trees, bomb craters, hidden ravines, and enemy mines all took a serious toll on the equipment, and occasionally on the equipment operators as well. But, as a highly reliable piece of heavy equipment, the Caterpillar D7E was often known to have gone well beyond the standard limitations of it's designed capabilities, while performing quite well in Vietnam, despite all of the obstacles that it ran up against. This too, to some extent, could be said for the operators of these machines, as they became skilled in maneuvering and avoiding various hazards in the course of working the cut. Their practical inventiveness at times had brought about solutions to certain immediate problems; and they too had occasionally weathered the conditions and exceeded their own expected capabilities, while enduring what the jungle had to throw at them during some of the more grueling days when the work within the environment's densely foliated landscape had seemed like much more than just a challenge.

When working in areas where large trees were sometimes more prevalent, with their wider trunks and higher canopies presenting a further challenge to the plow operators, it was quite common to see flying Lemurs gliding from tree to tree, as the rumble and roar of the plows, along with trees being toppled, had disturbed these monkey-like creatures to the point of screaming in dire protest as they glided out of harm's way from tree to tree, by stretching out their flabby excess furry skin in the form of an air-foil, to make their hasty yet forced retreat.

Despite the demanding nature and grueling hard work involved with a land clearing mission, it was simply routine for these men to spend 10 to12 hours working the cut, under adverse conditions in the jungle, before returning to the Night Defensive Position to spend another 6 or 8 hours while working into the night, pulling maintenance and making necessary repairs on their tractors, before having to repeat the whole process again on the very next day.

Barring all of the hardships and harsh conditions associated with the entire project, through their own self-sacrifice, it was always their driving desire to just keep going, until finally reaching the finish line on the 45th day of the operation; after which the land clearing unit would then pack everything back up again, while loading the plows onto the lowboy trailers, before heading back to their main basecamp for a 15-day maintenance standdown.

For the operation's roughly constructed night defensive position, its make-up featured a pushed-up circular berm of dirt surrounding it, 4 feet in height, serving as its topographically defined outline, and as the outside perimeter for the makeshift encampment. The mechanized security force that served as the unit's protectorate on these operations, had regularly positioned their tanks and armored personnel carriers (APCs) all around the perimeter of the compound at night, just inside the berm, to monitor the areas just outside the NDP, while helping to ensure that the encampment wouldn't get overrun at any time during the overnight hours by a sudden enemy ground attack.

At one end of this field compound, inside of where the mechanized security track vehicles were positioned, a large designated area was established by the LC unit's maintenance personnel to serve as a motor pool of sorts, where the plows and other equipment would gather around a diesel-powered air compressor at the end of the day, to blow out leaves and small branches with an air hose, along with the heavy accumulation of dust from the jungle, while also blowing out the tractor engine's air filter and the engine compartment. Plus, because the operators had also exhibited a significant amount of accumulated dust all over their bodies from the day's activities, they took turns with the air hose in helping to blow it all off of each other. At that time, the engine's oil level, and the water level for the radiator were routinely checked and re-plenished, if called for. The company's fuel truck driver would then come around with his 2 and a half ton tanker truck and hand the pump nozzle to the operator to fill up the tractor's diesel fuel tank that was positioned just below the back of the tractor's cab. This required the operator to climb up and stand firmly on the winch drum, in order to access the tank's fill spout. The use of a grease gun was also a common sight then, to add new grease to track roller fittings that sometimes went dry. Also at that time, if an operator may have detected a problem for a mechanic to check out, or for a welder to address, it was his responsi-bility to alert them while pointing things out.

Occasionally, belly-pans (*heavy steel shrouds that provided protection for the underside of both the engine and transmission*) had to be unbolted and dropped open by way of a hinge on one side, before cleaning out the potentially hazardous material within. The heavy steel protective pans had often contained compacted dried leaves and branches that would naturally work their way in through the pan's vent holes. If ignited by spontaneous combustion from the intense heat of the engine and loss of venting, a bellypan fire could often present a situation of serious concern, whereby the operator is then immediately obligated to somehow extinguish it before the flames advance further to burn up electrical wires and other components that would then put the plow on a hook headed back to the NDP for extensive repairs to the electrical system. Part of the difficulty with this little emergency had involved crawling underneath the tractor to get face to face with the situation while frantically trying to extinguish the flames as best as possible, as this was the only way to effectively apply a solution to the problem. It was always an exasperating chore for the operator to suddenly have to take on, given that the limited overhead space underneath the tractor only allowed for one to lay on their back while desperately trying to extinguish the fire with canteen cups of water drawn from a 5 gallon 'Jerry Can', or with what the immediate surroundings had provided, by simply resorting to smothering it with handfuls of dirt tossed in through the vent holes. In time, it was found that hand-pump type water cans with attached hoses, or even mounted gravity-feed type cans with hoses running down from them were more effective and much better suited for that occasional task.

As the nightly maintenance work went on, each Rome Plow blade at some point was raised up high enough to apply a pneumatic powered hand grinder to it, as the operator would commonly grind the beveled edge of the blade and the stinger, to routinely sharpen and renew its razor-like cutting edge, in preparation for the following day's continued engagement with the dense foliage of the jungle. Maintenance on all of the equipment tended to run well into the night, after everyone had eaten their evening meal, with many of the mechanics working under the lights right along with the operators. For this purpose, the NDP motor pool was always brightly lit, like a night baseball game at Dodger Stadium, (*or the ballpark of your choice*) in order to make it all possible. However, it always left that part of the NDP highly vulnerable at night to a potential rocket or mortar attack.

In the more centrally located area of the Night Defensive Position, near where the field mess area was set up, various sized canvas tents were positioned all around to house the land clearers, where a few sandbagged bunkers were also positioned here and there as immediate sources of refuge from the occasional incoming mortar and rocket fire. Short of putting in the work to create their own sandbagged bunkers, some of the plow operators would actually park their tractors right near their tent at night, to effectively use it as an impenetrable bunker of sorts, if needed. It seemed that these solid steel track vehicles when used in this way had offered much more protection underneath them than the sandbagged bunkers ever could. Although, the rear area beneath the plow had to be dug out somewhat to be able to use it as a bunker, in accessing it quickly and easily enough at night without accidentally banging one's head on solid steel during their frenzied scramble.

During the dry season, with the presence of mostly laterite type soil that was quite common in many of the areas within the central lowlands, the ground had been tested daily within the NDP by the inward and outbound traffic from the dozers and other vehicles; having been ground up and churned by the heavy tractors into a fine powdery beige-colored dust that often became rather thick and somewhat deeply coated in many areas of the compound with this quite dense accumulation of dust particulates. At times, it all looked much like heavy deposits of moon dust, which was quite strange to have to walk through, as it was somewhat fluffy and would often cover at least 2/3rds or more of the height of one's boots.

However, during the season of Monsoon, things were just the opposite, as the constantly saturated soil then became more of a deep muddy mess from the persistent precipitation and movements of the trucks and tractors each day. These conditions, while they tended to vary from place to place, often made it rather difficult to walk or trudge through without occasionally getting momentarily stuck in the sticky mud, depending on where you might be wandering within the motor pool area of the NDP. Although, unlike the aforementioned accumulation of dust, the mud tended to thickly cover and remain stuck to one's boots, giving a little more weight to one's gait, in getting around.

But with regard to the relentless heavy rains associated with the seasonal phenomena of Monsoon, the men found that during that period of the wet season it was next to impossible for them to keep clean and dry; especially when it came to one's feet, until removing most all of their clothing at night before catching some 'shut-eye' upon their cots. But, with the constant wet and muddy conditions that the men had to endure during the extreme unmerciful periods of Monsoon, one's boots were found on a daily basis, to be thoroughly caked with the sticky-gooey stuff.

Given that their Army issued jungle boots were not at all waterproof, the men were always left entirely wet clear through from the mud's saturation effect. The heavy laterite mud tended to cling to the entire form of each boot while transferring its watery content through the boot's leather and nylon fabric to completely soak one's socks, while keeping their feet in a constant state of wetness throughout the day, and leaving the wearer at high risk of developing Jungle Rot. Scraping the mud off of one's boots was about the best that could be done each night after finishing all of one's tasks prior to 'lights out', while having to do it all again on the following night. However, in the morning when putting the boots back on, they were still found to be at least damp at best, if not as fully saturated as they were on the previous day. Because of this thick mud having been present at times, all throughout the NDP, it just wasn't practical to build and install boardwalks to get around on while working. So, everyone just endured the muddy conditions as best as possible, while trying to avoid certain areas where greater depth would create a further challenge, and maybe even call for a change of fatigues.

For the land clearers in the two northern zones of South Vietnam, conditions were somewhat different, as the terrain tended to be considerably hilly and sloped for the areas where they worked. The ground there was comprised of a mix of both soil and rock, making Monsoon season much more treacherous and slippery to work in, while attempts to maintain solid traction on slopes with somewhat rocky inclines tended to present a further challenge to the plow operators.

During each night within the NDP, the security force

had routinely fired off aerial flares at different intervals, to illuminate areas just outside of the berm where movement may have been suspected. But with the popping of those flares every so often, along with the bright light that came with these slowly descending illuminators that floated down by way of small parachutes, it sometimes made it rather difficult for the land clearing personnel to maintain uninterrupted sleep. Although, that little annoyance was soon realized as something that went along with the territory, as everyone would agree that it was a very important aspect in helping to maintain the night security during these operations.

However, another major incident that would occasionally surprise the NDP encampment and immediately cut into everyone's nighttime slumber came in the form of mortars and rockets suddenly being fired into the compound by the Viet Cong or NVA forces, where their explosive ordinance would sometimes hit their marks and kill or injure a few of the men who may have still been sleeping in their tents. But, for those who could scramble out to their sandbag reinforced bunkers, or to effectively take refuge underneath their dozers, their levels of anxiety would soon diminish and they would then have to wait for an 'all clear' order before returning to possibly salvage what was left of their rudely interrupted night of sleep.

During the day, as the plows steadily worked the cut, the NDP site would occasionally be abandoned for another site down the road, nearer to where the plows had reached with their forward progress. (roughly after about every 7 to 10 days) At that time, everything would then be dismantled from how it was, folded and placed onto a lowboy trailer or into a deuce 'n half truck for transport to the next designated location where it would all be re-assembled again, as two bull blade dozers were busily carving out the new site in advance of them, while also pushing up a new circular earthen berm.

The day's cut was always carefully planned out during the previous evening by the security force commander, along with the supporting land clearing commander, while mapping out the area to be cleared. At that time, the two commanding officers would consider the terrain involved, and any possible hazards that could be problematic for the plows. Plus, consideration would be given to the setting of patterns for all of the track vehicles, with regard to the routes heading to and from the cut, in order to avoid possible land mines placed in their previously established paths. Additionally, they would consider, in the event where the enemy may have been found to be present inside of the targeted area to be cut, whether air strikes or artillery may be needed prior to sending in the plows to carve out the trace.

The PRC-25 field radio was commonly utilized during these operations as a direct means of communication between the security elements and Land Clearers who were monitoring the cut, to keep everyone apprised of all that may have been going on at any given moment. It had always served the operations well, in maintaining the close cohesiveness of the entire assembly of land clearing personnel, and each of the security's mechanized track vehicles, as these two-way radios tended to remain relatively trouble-free without many issues, to effectively keep everyone in communication and on the same page of the script, while helping to maintain the flow of the cut moving forward. At night within the operator's squad tents, the men would be obligated to take their turn every hour throughout the evening and early morning hours, standing 'Radio Watch', while using a helmeted headset to monitor and stay tuned-in with the mechanized security's overnight watch of the compound, while writing letters or reading to stay awake.

The land clearers, with their maintenance and parts trucks and other wheeled vehicles, had also maintained a Commo truck inside the compound, with a few personnel who regularly monitored the radio. But they were additionally capable of transmitting and receiving radio transmissions on a short wave band-width with their engineer unit in the rear, at their main basecamp many miles away, as well as with USARV command (*U.S. Army Republic of Vietnam*) at Long Binh Post. Also, when working in certain areas where hills and mountains were present or nearby, observation posts were temporarily established at these heights by a few members of the commo team, to report on any suspicious or unusual activity that might be of concern, while also serving as a relay point for any short wave radio transmissions. For this, a few members of the LC unit's limited security force had also been sent along, to help secure the observation post.

With regard to the start of activities involving the plows each day, the defining aspect of the cut had to do with establishing the area's trace, or the straight-line initial cut that commonly creates a square or rectangular outline for all of the other plows to follow and cut out concentrically, in counter-clockwise fashion, until all of the jungle growth in that defined sector had been cut down and eliminated. For this, an officer from the land clearing unit would routinely fly overhead in a light observation helicopter, while maintaining radio contact with the lead plow operator through the use of headsets. As the lead plow would advance and begin cutting, without being able to see anything except the dense jungle that the tractor was cutting through, the operator would maintain a straight directional cut while under the radio guidance of the officer above, in creating the outline or trace for the other plows to follow. At some point, the officer overhead would instruct the operator to make a 90 degree left turn and continue straight-on until another turn was called for. Eventually, with this method applied, the entire trace would then be completed, in establishing the basic outline by which the trailing tractors could then simply continue to follow along behind while cutting out the remaining foliage, to finally eliminate the entire square or rectangular defined sector of jungle before moving on to establish another trace to cut out.

In monitoring things on the move, the security's armored track vehicles would routinely follow the plows as closely as they were able, just out of range from falling trees, as the constant progression with the clearing process played out each day. But, quite often it was also necessary to help maintain proper access for these mechanized track vehicles, in order to keep them well within range of the plows in case of an attack of some sort, or if one of the plows were to hit a landmine with the operator in need of assistance, or any other possible scenario that would qualify as an emergency situation.

With all of the heavy debris and fallen trees lying about from the day's activities, the factory suspensions for these armored vehicles were noted to be somewhat limited in capability as compared with the dozers, making the haphazard terrain much too difficult to traverse without causing a serious break-down. So, by assigning one or two tractors to push some of the fallen trees and other downed debris aside every now and then, it allowed for safer passage for these combat vehicles, in order to help maintain their proper distance from the activity in the cut. This had effectively kept everyone well within close enough viewing range as they worked.

Generally, in the course of a day, it was common for one quarter to one third of the Rome Plows to sustain break-downs or disabling damage of some sort. Although, with much of this damage having been found to be minor, it was always repaired on the spot by a team of mechanics who would travel around the cut in a M548 maintenance track vehicle that contained vital parts and tools, and welding equipment, while often carrying a medic onboard as well. In other cases where issues with the plows could not be fixed on the spot, they would be towed back to the night defensive position where more time and attention could then be afforded to provide more involved and detailed repairs. In some cases where the operational area was often inaccessible by road, removal of the damaged or disabled equipment became somewhat complicated. But, with whatever the given circumstances, the land clearing engineers, in this type of scenario, would soon address the problem and figure out the best method of remedy. Occasionally, they would even make some major repairs in the field that were ordinarily done in the unit's main basecamp.

Although, despite some of the difficulties in repairing these tractors in the field, it wasn't entirely unusual to have one of these disabled Rome Plows hauled back into the operation's night defensive position, disassembled down to its very framework and re-fitted with new major parts and components, before being returned to service, back in the cut, in just a few days' time.

When it came to maintaining an inventory of needed parts for these dozers, the mechanics monitoring the cut from within their maintenance tracks had generally kept a lot of the more commonly used ones on hand for the types of repairs that were encounterd more often, in an overall effort to help keep the plows moving, if possible. Although, on a regular basis, more parts and seals, along with barrels of motor oil and transmission fluid and grease would be delivered almost daily to the NDP site by Chinook helicopters, as it became more of a routine practice in ensuring that the operation's mechanics remained well stocked with enough parts and other related materials that would aid in keeping the dozers operational and perpetually on the move. However, in other situations when certain parts were occasionally in short supply, mechanics would sometimes have to resort to cannibalizing a heavily damaged 'dead-lined' plow for some of its still useable parts, in order to again, help keep other downed tractors fully operational and moving forward.

As the plows continued to cut out the established trace, a platoon sergeant or squad leader was regularly positioned either within the M548 maintenance track, or upon one of the mechanized security's armored personnel carriers, seated just behind its driver, while equipped with an M-16 rifle and PRC-25 radio. For his role in this, he was to sit and monitor the cut, while also offering occasional assistance by way of radio communication with the security and the maintenance track, in the event of a break down or a possible issue involving the medic. At the end of each day, it was also his responsibility to round up all of the plows by signaling to the operators, before escorting them in single file back to the NDP.

Considering the type of work being done and the potential hazards that were directly involved with it, along with occasional encounters with the enemy, high casualty rates for a land clearing unit were expected. Most of the enemy-involved casualties were directly attributed to the presence of land mines, booby traps, small arms fire, and the firing of rocket propelled grenades (RPG's) in and around the cut, along with mortar and B-40 rocket attacks that targeted the land clearers' night defensive positions during the evening or overnight hours. Conversely, many of the other 'natural' type hazards where casualties had resulted, were attributed to serious accidents, which occasionally came from large falling trees, and from tractor roll-overs where there were unseen obstacles in the operator's path; or as a result of working in hilly terrain where an operator may have gotten too close to the edge of a ravine.

But, one of the more notable and problematic among the various natural hazards in the jungle was the southeast Asian Bee, as swarms of these stinging insects sometimes brought the clearing activity to a standstill when their hives were stirred up. Many of the affected operators had to be evacuated to field hospitals for treatment and recovery, as some of them were left in serious condition after having been stung multiple times by these often angry and aggressive Bees, which appeared to be a little bit larger in size than the standard honey bee back in the states. Interestingly, it was found that the use of green smoke grenades actually worked quite well in repelling the little flying demons; although, nobody ever knew why, as no other colored smoke had the same effect on these potentially dangerous little bugs like the green smoke had. So, plow operators were often reminded to keep several of the grenade-like cannisters on hand within their cabs.

In situations where one or more of the plow operators had sustained an injury of some sort where they could not continue with their assigned task on any given day, an equipment mechanic from the maintenance track vehicle would sometimes be called on to take over the plow and act as a substitute for the remainder of the day.

On a daily basis when clearing the various types of growth existing within the cut, a land clearing unit could be expected to clear anywhere between 150 to 200 acres of medium jungle. But with a number of different variables involved, considering the weather and terrain, along with maintenance issues and enemy encounters, the numbers can be adversely affected. Also, the numbers tended to drop considerably when the plows were cutting in heavy growth type forests with larger trees involved. However, to help speed up production, some of the different land clearing units had involved themselves in a prideful sort of competition at one point during 1968, to see which one had the most productive numbers over the course of time, as they found that it was a way for the plow operators to measure their skills alongside those of another 'sister' unit, whereby the platoon leaders had access to the production reports for these units, and tended to use them to spur on their operators. Although, when it was noted that the plows were then experiencing ever increasing break downs and added maintenance issues, it had suddenly put a stop to that ill-advised practice.

Over the short course of only a few years' time after applying the amazing effectiveness of the Rome Plow tractor to the Vietnam landscape, in opening up many of the densely forested areas of jungle where the Viet Cong had formerly established their bases of operation, the openly assertive land clearing tactics were then showing more positive and promising signs of success.

The unexpected interdiction of some of these enemy bases found within the jungle, which contained elaborate underground tunnels in many cases, along with key connecting trails and routes where their supplies had formerly flowed, had left the Viet Cong in a situation where they then had to constantly adjust, in trying to deal with the ongoing disappearance of their highly revered jungle cover that had previously served them so well, while successfully launching their covert operations from a seemingly undetectable forward base, within a forested area of dense tropical growth.

These smartly designed systems of underground tunnels, when discovered by the land clearers and/or the mechanized security forces, were found to often feature connecting rooms where dry stores of food were regularly kept in reserve, along with weapons and ammunition; and where enemy soldiers would routinely sleep and eat at times, while other rooms had also served as a refuge where some of their sick or wounded would be brought in to be cared for.

Their well-crafted tunnels were dug out in such a way to effectively keep them from collapsing, as the passageways were carved out from compacted naturally rich iron and aluminum laterite soil, with the passageways designed to be vertically oval in shape instead of round, while many of the connecting rooms had also featured earthen pillar type supports in some cases, to help maintain the inner integrity of these cave-like subterranean earthen structures.

However, from the Army Corps of Engineer's view of things, with the overall improvement in security where allied soldiers were more and more able to gain greater line of sight as a result of these land clearing missions, it allowed them to actually see and react to the enemy from time to time, as it provided them with more of a sense of relief while making their jobs somewhat easier than it was when all of the jungle cover was formerly in place. What was once previously known as enemy territory had suddenly represented a measure of great progress. This observation was not only noted in a military sense, but also in terms of pacification and local economic development, as mentioned previously, which clearly showed that a revitalization throughout the countryside had been realized to some extent, with new agricultural opportunities springing up where dense jungle had once stood; even while a war was still ongoing. Also, traffic on the formerly troubled roadways had come alive again after the Viet Cong's jungle cover was effectively removed, with their formerly invincible threat of roadside ambushes having finally been dealt with and effectively thwarted.

Aerial view of a cut-out area within a densely wooded jungle

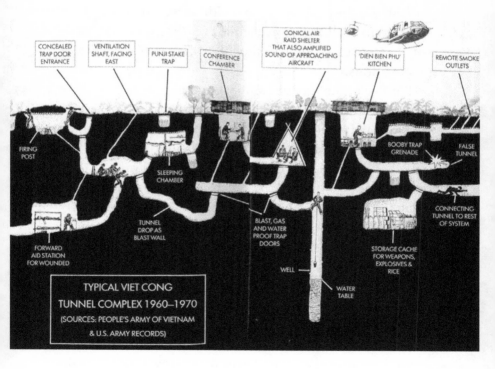

CONCEALED TRAP DOOR ENTRANCE

VENTILATION SHAFT, FACING EAST

PUNJI STAKE TRAP

CONFERENCE CHAMBER

CONICAL AIR RAID SHELTER THAT ALSO AMPLIFIED SOUND OF APPROACHING AIRCRAFT

'DIEN BIEN PHU' KITCHEN

REMOTE SMOKE OUTLETS

FIRING POST

SLEEPING CHAMBER

BOOBY TRAP GRENADE

FALSE TUNNEL

FORWARD AID STATION FOR WOUNDED

TUNNEL DROP AS BLAST WALL

BLAST, GAS AND WATER PROOF TRAP DOORS

WELL

WATER TABLE

STORAGE CACHE FOR WEAPONS, EXPLOSIVES & RICE

CONNECTING TUNNEL TO REST OF SYSTEM

TYPICAL VIET CONG TUNNEL COMPLEX 1960–1970
(SOURCES: PEOPLE'S ARMY OF VIETNAM & U.S. ARMY RECORDS)

These key examples which reflect strongly on some of the overall successes that came as a direct result of the application of land clearing tactics in South Vietnam, were achieved through what was made possible with the practical use of the 'great experiment', otherwise known as the Rome Plow tractor. Its tactical use had also brought about more of those same type results in other areas of the country during the few remaining years of land clearing operations in the latter part of the Vietnam war, up until the U.S. forces' incremental withdrawal from the country by way of a planned phase-down.

But for all that was accomplished and all that was gained through the application of land clearing in Vietnam, it was the engineer corps soldiers who had sacrificed so much for so little regard, while enduring constant hardships and even tragedies when working on these dangerous missions.

For these courageous combat engineers, in seeing their operations through and bringing them to their eventual conclusion, it took a team effort to make it all possible, as there were several different key contributing factors involved with each land clearing unit's overall makeup. To ensure that everything would actually work according to design, these well-coordinated land clearing operations had to be aligned together as a working system, with all of their various personnel and equipment coming together in an almost choreographed way to contribute as one element, in becoming an effective and efficient engineer tactical force. Otherwise, to put it plainly and quite simply, it just wouldn't have worked as effectively as it did.

But, for all of their gritty efforts in helping to facilitate these operations and to clear away the jungle while improving on security within the country, a price was paid, with many of these young men having sustained serious injuries and wounds during the process; while an even higher price was paid by the loss of many others who had been killed while working these land clearing missions. These men, who are listed as Killed in Action, had served quite admirably in the various Land Clearing units, while putting in their best efforts in performing the required tasks associated with their job placement, up until the sudden moment of their sad departure. Their names, now permanently etched in stone upon the wall monument in Washington, DC, known more prominently as the Vietnam Veteran's Memorial, remain as an ongoing testament to their selfless sacrifice as Land Clearing Combat Engineers of the U.S. Army.

Devil's Advocate

Purely from a 'Devil's Advocate' position on the subject, by allowing one of land clearing's more outspoken critics of the period to give his opinion on the Rome Plow's overall application in South Vietnam, as someone in a high position of prominence who obviously had little understanding about the saving of countless lives through the implementation of the clearing process, Richard Anderson Faulk, a leading professor of international law and a notable opponent of the Vietnam war, wrote in 1973:

"I think it is not easy to conclude that Rome plowing, however much it offends ecological consciousness, constitutes a violation of existing standards of international law." Citing post-World War II indictments against nine German officials who had overseen "the wholesale cutting of Polish timber to an extent far in excess of what was necessary to preserve the timber resources of the country", however, he also concluded that "it is possible to view such environmental devastation as an instance of 'a crime against humanity' in the Nuremberg sense."

The Rome Plow K/G Blade

Ernest Kissner owned and operated draglines in Lottie, Louisiana; an area about 75 miles west of Baton Rouge. Since this type of work kept him away from home and family quite a bit, he counseled with his father-in-law, Ed Greene, sometime in the early 1950's, in reminding him that he owned more land than he could possibly take care of by himself. As a result, Mr. Greene was willing to sell off some of this land to Kissner on a long-term basis with the provision that Kissner clear the land for pasture and croplands.

So, Kissner purchased a bulldozer and an angle blade and started attacking the heavy Louisiana jungle-like growth in the conventional manner... that is, by cutting the tree roots, pushing the trees over and dozing them out. While doing the work himself as the operator, he decided there had to be a better way to go about it; especially on springy, ash tree thickets. After further counseling together with his father, John Kissner, Sr. and his father-in-law Ed Greene, he decided that a knife-like cutting edge attached to the bulldozer blade would be a more practical solution, but found this only worked on the smaller diameter ash and similar type trees. After shearing this type of growth off level with the ground, he would then have to remove his cutting edge and go back to conventional grubbing of the larger trees with a bull blade.

One day it dawned on him that he could actually speed up work and save money if he could whittle larger trees down to size and then shear them off at ground level, leaving the roots in place. From this idea he then developed the now familiar "Stinger" or splitter which he attached to the custom dozer blade by welding it at the left side of the leading edge, and then started experimenting.

He found that the combination of a splitter and shearing blade when applied together had dramatically reduced the work and time of operation considerably, while drastically reducing the cost.

He also discovered that he could use the same tool for windrowing the cut material, thereby saving the time required to change from the cutting blade back to the conventional dozer bull blade or rake that he had previously used for windrowing. Plus, he found by cutting the trees flush with the ground he could windrow this material with less dirt going into the windrow piles than by conventional methods done with a bull blade.

When discovering that their original idea had substantially reduced the overall cost of land clearing, along with the time involved with its use on the landscape, the parties associated with the development of it, immediately filed for patents.

As word spread about this cost and time reducing tractor attachment, Kissner was soon deluged with requests from pipe liners, highway contractors and land developers to clear land for them on a contract basis.

But it quickly became apparent that he couldn't possibly take care of all this work, even with a sizable fleet of tractors. He therefore, started manufacturing attachments consisting of the cutting edge, the stinger and brush guards which he sold to individual contractors for them to self-install.

Faced with the constantly growing requirements for larger production facilities, and having little experience in manufacturing, he sought out an established firm, The Rome Plow Company of Cedartown, Georgia, to manufacture and distribute the now patented Rome K/G Blade on a royalty basis.

Since signing the agreement in October, 1957, thousands of the Rome K/G Blades have been clearing land all over the world. For this purpose, there is nothing else that can touch this unit for quick and economical land clearing which at the same time leaves the top soil in place and eliminates the problem of stump holes and root balls. With this simple but exceedingly important tool put to use, some of the unproductive jungles of the earth have effectively been transformed into crop lands, to feed the ever-increasing population of the world. In Vietnam the U. S. Army Corps of Engineer's use of Rome K/G Blades had helped to clear out enemy strongholds and ambush sites, while turning many heavily jungled target areas into what are now productive crop lands.

The following is an excerpt from Ernest Kissner's November 2006 obituary, highlighting some of his little-known achievements prior to inventing the K/G blade:

Kissner, James Ernest; A retired contractor, rancher and co-inventor of the KG clearing blade, died Saturday, Nov. 18, 2006, at 7 a.m. in Opelousas at Doctor's Hospital. He was 86, a resident and native of Lottie, Louisiana and a U.S. Air Force B-29 veteran pilot of World War II.

He joined the Army Air Corps at age 22 and flew missions in World War II. He served as 1st lieutenant with the

355th Bombardment Squadron and 331st Bombardment Group; flew B-17s and B-29s; flew 13 air campaigns over Japan and flew in the last air mission of the war over Japan. He received the Air Medal, Asiatic Pacific Campaign Medal with Two Bronze Stars, American Campaign Medal, World War II Victory Medal, the Presidential Unit Citation with One Oak Leaf Cluster and was presented with a Presidential Testimonial.

He had a passion for animals, land clearing, bulldozers, and cypress trees.

Given his date of death, it clearly appears that Ernest Kissner had lived to realize just how well the Army Corps of Engineers and all of South Vietnam had greatly benefitted from the use of his thoughtful invention.

Rome Plow K/G Blade

U.S. Army Air Corps B-29 Bomber

The Stories

SP/5 Dennis Hall

595th Light Equipment Company
Wheel and Track Vehicle Mechanic
1966 – 1967
Hometown: Dallas, Texas

Bearcat

The 595th Light Equipment Company left Fort Riley, Kansas in Late March of 1966 for Viet Nam. We traveled out to Oakland, California, by train, arriving in Oakland in early February at the docks, ready to board the USNS Gen. Weigel, an old troop ship. It was a frigid trip from there; then it started getting warmer the farther south we went. The pores in my skin were so closed up that sweat could not get out, and big water blisters came up mostly on my arms.

Aboard ship, we were herded into small compartments with hammock-type racks about four high. The second or third day out, we ran into storm-related heavy swells that rocked the ship up and down very badly. Every time we went down, you could hear the screws (propellers) whirring when coming out of the water, while many of the men onboard were busy puking up everything because of the extreme up and down motion. In the galley, you could hardly eat for the smell of vomit. I tried to spend as much time out on deck as possible.

About two and a half weeks later, we pulled into Subic Bay Naval Base in the Philippines. We were there about two days before sailing out to Viet Nam, where we first landed at Da Nang and let a bunch of men off, and then sailed down off the coast of Vung Tau, where we went over the side on Jacobs Ladders and onto a landing craft that took us to about a hundred yards off the beach and dumped us. I had two duffle bags and my rifle that I had to hold over my head; the water was neck-deep, and I was five foot eleven. After we reached shore, we were loaded onto 'deuce and half' (2 & ½ ton open bed) trucks for our trip over to the Ninetieth Replacement Company in Bien Hoa, which was where almost all Army personnel within the III Corps tactical zone had initially checked-in for processing when arriving in country, prior to getting assigned to their new unit and/or location.

We were there about three days before convoying up to Camp Black Horse where we stayed temporarily with the Eleventh Armored Cavalry Regiment, commanded by Col. George Patton Jr. While there, we received mortar attacks almost every night. I remember the first night we were in our tent, and the horns started blaring, and we were told that the horns sounding meant for everyone to head for a bunker. A defined bunker there was just a trench about three feet deep covered with rubber tree logs. Still, one thing I recall from hunkering down in that bunker was that everyone I could hear nearby was saying a prayer, including myself. For my part, I was telling God I would be a better person if He would get me out of this predicament, and He did... and I tried to be.

Sadly, while there at Blackhorse, our First Sergeant had suffered a heart attack and died. Several days past, as we were still waiting on our equipment to arrive. So, we were just killing time while also waiting for assignment. Then, from there we were transported south to Camp Bearcat, where we were then set up in a permanent basecamp within the compound, as the 595th Light Equipment Company had then joined with the 86th Engineer Battalion there, to serve as a battalion detachment.

In addition to being the HQ for the 86th, Bearcat was also the main base camp for the 9th Infantry Division at that time. Our new location was about ten miles southeast of Bien Hoa, where we found to our relief that we didn't suffer as many mortar attacks there. The 86th Engineer Battalion at that time, had also previously established a Land Clearing Platoon.

When we first got there, I worked the motor pool as a dispatcher, which had gotten to be very dull. I wanted to be out in the field, and kept bugging my motor pool sergeant to replace me and put me in the field instead, saying that I could do better there than in the motor pool, given that I had been working on cars and trucks since I was in the eighth grade, and I was already well versed on how mechanical equipment worked. Finally, my day came, as a man in our unit was recommended for the DSC for heroism, and they didn't want him to remain in the field where he might otherwise receive it posthumously.

So, I suggested that he be made dispatcher, and I would get a mechanics truck and go out in the field to replace him. The suggestion worked, and I loved it! I got to go all over the south part of our operations area. I especially remember that I had to go down to Dong Tam, in the Delta, to work on a dragline, and because the work ran me late into the day, I wound up getting stuck there overnight. Unknowingly, I had parked my truck too close to a big gun called 'Long Tom', which fired a humongous long-range round over into Cambodia, and every time they would fire it, the resulting concussive effect from it would rock my truck sideways. So, I didn't get much sleep, if at all that night.

The next day, after my work there was finished, I was bent on heading back to Bearcat and positioned the truck for the return trip while lining it up in a line of vehicles to convoy out. But there weren't enough vehicles assembled to get the OK to go, so I sat there for about an hour to allow time for the convoy to build, and there still weren't enough assembled there to leave. So, I went back to the club to drink a beer, and just while-away some of the time while hoping the convoy would increase in size, in order to make it large enough to fully warrant the company-size protection provided by the available mechanized security unit. But when returning I found that the convoy had left while I was in there, which was disappointing, to say the least. But I was mainly mad, thinking that I was going to have to listen to that big gun again that night.

The following day I drove over to the staging area and lined up again. While sitting there, a sergeant walked up and told me that the convoy that left yesterday had been all wiped out between there and Saigon, and every last man was killed. While I naturally felt shocked and saddened to hear that news, I also felt a whole lot better about having missed that convoy, although I suddenly felt a bit shaky and uncertain about joining up with this one.

My guardian angel was apparently looking after me, as I'm sure he knew that I liked beer. The next time something like that happened, I was at Gia Rai working on a dozer, and I was supposed to convoy back, before another Caterpillar D7-E broke down. So, I had to stay and didn't make that day's convoy back either, as a result. However, as it turned out, they too were ambushed, and many were killed.

While there at Gia Rai, the word was put out that about twelve hundred VC had surrounded us, and we were placed on high alert and confined to our bunkers. We were told that no one was supposed to sleep, and if anyone was caught napping, they would be court-martialed.

That night the VC began to attack, and a chopper called Jolly Green Giant (*a type of attack helicopter*) came in and started firing its miniguns as the VC advanced from outside the perimeter, with those rapid-fire guns mowing down all who were in sight. We were kind of scared at the time because there were only about six APCs in the compound and maybe just a hundred other troops, including engineers. After Jolly left, 'Puff the Magic Dragon' (*A modified fixed-wing aircraft*) came in with their miniguns roaring.

"Puff" was actually a World War II AC-47 converted cargo plane, equipped with three miniguns on the left side of the aircraft. With all of the rapid-fire displays, this was better than the fourth of July. After that, everything died down and nothing else happened the rest of the night.

The following day we had C-rations for breakfast and remained in the bunker. I was ranking man in the bunker, so I went over to see what was going on, and was told there were still plenty of VC in the area, and that we were still on high alert and needed to stay in the bunker, with strict orders to only get out to go to the latrine, while we were still due to get in about a hundred or more men and some supplies, brought in by chopper.

Because of the situation, we didn't have much water

available at the time, and the choppers couldn't risk things with the enemy activity in the area in order to re-supply us with the wet stuff, along with whatever else they were bringing in. But there were plenty of cases of beer on hand. So, we were each issued a can of beer about every three hours or so to make sure we didn't get intoxicated. As it turned out, not much else happened that day. The APCs simply moved to better strategic positions, and as the activity had died down, that was it for that day.

While I was there, a guy told me a story about this other man who had a pet monkey tied to a tree beside his bunk with enough rope to go in and out of the tent. The thing about it is that the monkey would come in and crap on the guy's cot that was next to his master's. The man whose bunk was getting crapped on told the owner he would kill the monkey the next time it happened. At some point he came in, and sure enough, there was monkey crap on his bunk again; so, he hung the monkey and killed it. When the owner then came in to find his monkey dead, he got his M-16, and shot and killed the monkey killer. I later found out that this was actually a true story, with the monkey's owner having been sent to serve his confinement for that deed to LBJ (Long Binh Jail), which was the Army's notorious military prison in South Vietnam. But I'm sure that when we finally left Vietnam in the final phase-out, he most likely was transferred to a stateside federal military prison like Leavenworth, to serve out the remainder of his days for that unfortunate lapse in judgement.

Well, back to the bunker. Fortunately, as suggested, we had received about a hundred reinforcements that day who had been flown in, and this made us feel a lot better, but we still didn't know how many VC were out there.

That night a Huey helicopter flew out in front of us about three hundred feet in the air, drawing fire, and managed to pinpoint their location. The 'Jolly Green Giant' modified assault helicopter then came in again, killing all in sight, as they couldn't hide from those overwhelming miniguns. But all in all, after that was over, everything was pretty quiet and still for the rest of that night.

The next day it looked like all was clearing up. We received more C-Rations for breakfast, but the mess hall was opening again, and it looked like we were going to get a hot meal. I finally got to work on the dozer and then afterward got situated in a convoy headed back to Bearcat.

My next assignment was located out on a Rome Plow cut, and while there, I learned that fellow 595th company mate Carlus Rutledge and his dozer had fallen into a notable depression that uncovered a VC underground tunnel complex. So, as the VC had already left and were nowhere to be found, I volunteered to help by going down into the tunnels and bringing out numerous rifles and other related materials. Among the items that were brought up, were a lot of American WWII rifles, various medicines from the Korean war, and all kinds of ammo. That discovery turned out to be the largest cache found, up to that point in time.

Most every night inside the circular bermed Night Defensive Positions that were established on these traces, we would pull four dozers in to form a square and put a steel plate over the top of the blades and sleep underneath, while the battleship New Jersey offshore would shoot their big sixteen-inch shells around us. It was a lot of noise, but we were so tired it didn't hardly faze us. I had received the Army Commendation Medal for helping on this operation, and I also got to bring one of the rifles back home with me.

While back at Bearcat, I had to take a dragline up to Bien Hoa for repairs; and while driving up there, I was coming head-on with a tank, and he wasn't going to give way, so I figured it was better for me to move over instead. While I was driving on, I kept hearing this honking behind me. Suddenly, I swerved to the right, and when I did, the rear outrigger on my maintenance truck swung out and caught a small truck sitting beside the road in this little village; and when I looked over, the truck was going into the river.

When I got up to my turn-off, a jeep pulled up beside me, and this Lieutenant asked me if I couldn't hear his horn. I said yes, and he wondered why I didn't stop. I told him I had orders never to stop outside of a compound; and that if he wanted, he could take it up with my C.O. In response, he just glared at me and walked off.

One day I was going to the P. X. at Tan Son Nhut Air Base in Saigon, and there were air police posted at the door. As I approached, they stopped me at the door and said I could not enter because my boots weren't shined. I told them that I had been out in the field a couple of weeks and hadn't had a chance to polish them, and surprisingly they understood and let me go ahead. But that just illustrates how 'statside' some of the larger posts in-country were, compared to posts like Bearcat.

One of the worst things I remember was driving through Saigon and the fish markets there. Even my gas mask didn't help cut the smell any. This awful fish smell and the smell of dead rotting human bodies will always haunt my senses whenever I think about it. 'Nuff said.

On another job assignment, we were building an airfield down by Vung Tau, and I had gone down to work on the roller, and when I was on my way back, an ammo truck was stranded along the road, so I stopped to help them and got them started up again, as they told me they were beginning to get worried about darkness coming on. So, I followed them on into Bearcat.

The men that usually were with me on my truck were John Chance from South Carolina and a man named Barbados. I can't remember his first name, although I recall that he was from Maui, Hawaii. Both were outstanding workers; I couldn't have asked for any better help. They were both worried about all the C-4 explosives that I carried in the truck, but to help calm their worries I told them we had to have it in order to heat our C-Rations to allow us to have a hot meal. Plus, in most cases, a blasting cap would have to be applied for the stuff to actually explode. Although, it didn't make them feel any better to know that if my truck had ever received a direct hit, there would be a big hole left in the ground.

That related incident reminds me of a time out on a Rome Plow trace when I took some C-4 and put it under my c-ration can, and started to stick a match to it, as this guy standing behind me jumped about ten feet. Not fully versed with the use of this stuff, he didn't know you had to have a blasting cap to make C-4 explode.

I had to go out one day to see if I could figure out what the problem was with this Le Tourneau tree crusher that had just started clearing acreage about a month earlier.

It was a big heavy monster of a machine with giant elongated star-shaped steel wheels, which was designed in a straight forward way, to run over trees and brush and simply crush them instead of cutting and pushing the debris aside. From my observations, while this machine was impressively effective in knocking down the jungle and crushing the trees as they lay, it didn't really work all that well in covering substantial acreage on a daily basis, as it just couldn't keep up with the Caterpillar D7E Rome Plows. Plus, it lacked the mobility factor in moving it from place to place, as it had to be partly disassembled for transport.

The name 'Rome', as it pertained to the Rome Plow tractors, actually comes from Rome, Georgia, where the plow blades were originally made, so I was told. In the course of things, we had one Rome Plow operator killed while I was there. His name was Moser, and I don't know the first name. He was from Austin, Texas. The dozer he operated was so badly damaged that it was dead-lined and deemed as not being salvageable for any further use, except to keep in order to cannibalize it for some of its still useable parts.

In recalling things about the TET Offensive, I was on the bunker as sergeant of the guard one night, and because I had a starlight scope, I found myself constantly running between bunkers every time someone thought they saw something. At that time, these nifty night vision devices were a relatively new thing, as they were found to be quite useful in actually seeing the enemy's movements in total darkness. However, not every soldier had one.

But, one stupid thing happened that night, as one of the men in the bunkers was bitten by a rat. Now mind you, these rats were nearly half the size of opossums. I asked him how he got bit, and he told me how this rat would keep running back and forth between the bunker gun opening; and he said he got tired of that and stuck his finger out to trip the rat, and the rat bit his finger, so he had to go to the aid station and get a bunch of shots. *Hey, I'm not making this stuff up.*

Coincidentally, I was scheduled to go home during the time of the TET offensive, but my flight was canceled, and I had to wait. Finally, as they were flying Air Force C-141 transport planes in, instead of the commercial Boeing 707's, I was placed on one of those flights. It's quite different than your conventional type airline experience, as you sit facing backwards in nylon netting hanging from the ceiling. Our deluxe onboard meals were C-rations, of course, and our first stop was in Guam, where we had to exit the plane while they refueled; and annoyingly, we all had to walk about half a mile up the tarmac to the terminal to wait there until they were ready to take off again. We were all wearing our short sleeve khaki uniforms at the time, and the outside temperature was about forty degrees there.

When we were taking off after refueling, the plane suddenly blew an engine, and it barely stopped just before we reached the end of the runway. To add to our anxiety, we noticed when deplaning again that there was a very steep cliff at the end of the runway where many planes had previously gone off and crashed. So, that was a little unsettling for all of us, to say the least. But as this situation had presented itself, we then found ourselves stuck with having to wait even longer, until the engine was replaced and tested, before we could finally take off again.

Next, we landed at Hickam Field in Hawaii, just long enough to refuel; and the next stop after that was at Travis Air Force Base in northern California, about thirty-five miles northwest of San Francisco. At the time, there were many hippies and other hyper-emotional dead-beat types there at Travis, who showed up to protest and try to torment us after we got off the plane. I had perceived them as the scum of the earth because of their seething hatred shown towards us, even though they didn't know us from 'Adam'. They were constantly hollering expletives and various uncomplimentary names in our direction, like "Murders" and "Baby Killers", as we were waiting in-transit there at the airport, while only interested in trying to get home.

With more bad luck, I somehow managed to miss my flight from there; so I had to resort to sleeping on the floor prior to catching another flight out the next day. But the hippies didn't mess with me there because I had my souvenir rifle that I brought back from 'Nam securely slung over my shoulder.

On the following day I finally caught my flight out to Dallas, and I was sure glad to get home.

That's my story, and I am sticking to it.

SP/4 John Walker

B Co, 26th Engineers – Americal Division, 23rd Infantry
1970 - 1971
Radio Operator
Hometown: Ruthven, Iowa

Onions

Years ago, on my blog as the River Rat Ranger, I posted this war story.... thought I'd share it: The year... 1970. The place.... several kilometers southeast of My Lai 4 on the peninsula south of Chu Lai, Vietnam. As the RRR, I was the radio operator for a Land Clearing Platoon. We had 4 bull dozers to uncover enemy tunnels and bunkers with, and enough personnel to operate, maintain, and protect them. We had established a "night laager" site on top of a hill that we operated from.

But we were hungry, desperately hungry for fresh vegetables. For 6 weeks we'd lived exclusively on C-rations, which were Army canned and packaged individual meals, although we absolutely craved fruits and vegetables. Each time I called the rear support area with the Lieutenant's daily report and equipment requests, I practically begged for fresh food. Finally, the opportunity came to contact the rear "secure". Part of my involved equipment was what was at that time a top-secret scrambling device for the radio. It was huge, heavy, unreliable, and absolute magic, which allowed me to talk to our company headquarters "in the clear" without using code, to actually communicate freely. As a measure of how seriously the secrecy surrounding this equipment was taken, I was issued a .45 caliber pistol and a thermite grenade with orders to destroy it if the situation called for it, in order to prevent it from falling into enemy hands, and to kill myself with the firearm if captured, so as to prevent any information about it from getting out by way of torture. I had no difficulty with the idea of following the latter orders. I'd seen the remains of soldiers who had been questioned by the Vietcong and had absolutely no desire to share their experience.

In the clear, I demanded over the scrambler that we be sent some fresh food. The First Sergeant got on the radio and explained to me that there had been a hold up in shipments for the entire division, not just us, but that they would assuredly send us SOMETHING.

So, we anxiously awaited the next resupply helicopter. Upon arrival, along with our mail, ammo, and tractor repair parts, the helicopter crew chief tossed out a wooden crate of fresh onions. It was all they had. The mess Sergeant had even included four pounds of butter to fry them up with. As the chopper departed, we stood around half dumbfounded, just staring at the crate of onions. I peeled the skin off of one and began eating it like an apple. But the Lieutenant had a sudden idea... "Let's make onion rings!" And make onion rings we did.

Soon, two of the men were busy slicing the onions. Another dug through the box of cast offs from the C-ration packs, digging out every powdered cream packet along with the ones containing salt and pepper. We crushed "hard tack", the Army crackers, and mixed that with water, along with powdered cream and spices to make a batter.

The demolition man opened a case of C-4 plastic explosive and burned a quarter stick inside of an empty .50 caliber ammo can to cook the paint out. That ammo can had then effectively become our French fryer. For a fry basket we took a tall quart and a half juice can and tactfully perforated it with a clip full of ammo from an M-16.

To round it out, a simple piece of wire from a C-ration crate made for the bail on our "fry basket". We placed the ammo can up on 4 rocks, put the butter in it and started burning little dabs of C-4 under it to melt and heat the butter. The onion rings were dipped in the batter and then placed in the basket that dropped into the hot butter. An M-16 rifle made a handy stick to hang the fry basket from.

They were DELICIOUS! The dozen or so of us ate onion rings and ate onion rings and ate onion rings. We devoured the entire crate. We ate 'till we were as full as ticks. It was 5 years before I could contemplate eating onion rings again. But that night, that one night, I ate all I wanted.

SP/4 Charlie "Slick" Allen

27th Land Clearing Team & 60th Land Clearing Company
("Jungle Eaters")
1968 – 1969
Rome Plow Operator
Hometown: Waterford, Michigan

Slick from Motown

My name is Charlie Kuron Allen, aka "Slick."

I was born on August 31, 1949. No one had told me there was a war in Vietnam. I joined the Army in October 1966 at Little Rock, Arkansas.

I was then shipped out to Ft. Polk, LA, for Basic Training. Previously, I had married a friend who was a victim of rape and had a six-week-old son. I told the County Clerk that he was my child and gave him my name. I joined the Army so Sharon and the baby could receive an allotment.

After Basic Training, I got to go home on a 30-day leave for Christmas. Then I was ordered to report to Ft. Lewis, WA, for AIT (Advanced Individual Training). I divorced in late-1967 and shipped out to Vietnam, as I was then heartbroken that my girlfriend had broken it off just two days before leaving. So, I helped myself to an additional 30-days of unauthorized leave (AWOL), then hopped on a flight to Ft. Houston, Texas before hitchhiking to Lepanto,

AR, to see my mom and siblings.

After that I went to Blytheville Air Force Base and got a travel voucher to San Francisco, where I was quickly forgiven for my 30-days of AWOL and ordered to go directly to Vietnam.

I arrived in-country on January 7, 1968. Initially, placed as a carpenter attached to the 62nd Engineer Battalion in Long Binh. That job placement was short-lived, and I alternately became a minesweeper, and then was given the opportunity to drive a 5-ton Dump Truck.

As I settled in, I learned to smoke pot and drink beer while continuing to nurse my broken heart. In October 1968 I was granted leave, and again came back 30-days late.

When I returned and visited the Enlisted Men's Club at Long Binh Post, I noticed that I only had $3.00 to my name. But I still managed to buy a round of beers for some of my friends, at $0.15 each. After finishing my beer, I went back to the company area to take a shower, and then walked toward my friend Paxton's hootch. Suddenly as I entered, something hit me on my head from behind and knocked me to the floor. I rolled over, and this guy Porky, with a straight razor to my throat, was threatening to kill me. My friend who was with me somehow got the razor from him in the scuffle, but as Porky fell on me, the impact bashed my head into the concrete floor where it wound up fracturing my skull. Long story short, as Porky and I had issues and clearly didn't get along, I told Top I was going to kill him. So, after a few days recuperating, I was subsequently transferred out of the 62nd and placed with the 27th Land Clearing Task Force where I had my first encounter with SSG Kirkpatrick. I never saw Porky again, which was a good thing for him.

SSG Kirkpatrick and I developed a poor relationship from the start. I never understood why he singled me out from time to time. Maybe because I was a pothead, and when the unit was on stand down, I drank Jack Daniels and got into fights at the EM Club. But I think I performed my job well enough as I could, considering.

I was a SP/4 when I got to the 27th and was assigned to operate Rome Plow #37. My adopted nickname was "Slick", because I seemed to have somewhat of a knack for sliding right through most any problem that was encountered. For the plow, I nicknamed it *"Slick from Motown"* because I lived in Detroit during my teen years from 14 to 17.

When attempting to operate the Rome Plow for the first time, Sergeant Kirkpatrick impatiently waited for me to crank up the machine and get going. Not being all that well versed on this piece of equipment, I struggled trying to figure out how to start it; so, someone came over and started it up for me. I then followed Dave "Corky" Ellis out to the rubber plantation, where the 'cut' was established at that time, while jerking the plow to the left and right when pulling on the steering clutches and tapping the brake pedals, as I managed to figure out how to steer it. This was late December in 1968, and Corky dragged me around the Michelin Rubber Plantation for about four hours that day, while we were both hooked up to a ship's anchor chain held by each tractor's rear draw pins, which I noticed was quite effective in pulling down rows of rubber trees behind us as we went; while he just laughed his ass off, in making fun of this newbie plow operator, as I slowly learned the ropes.

By 1100 hours, I was getting the hang of it and continued pulling the anchor chain with Corky for a few days thereafter. From there, I was then sent out on my own to join with the other plows in the regular version of the 'cut', where dense jungle was to be cut down with an unusual sharpened blade mounted on the front of the tractor that was angled or canted to the right side, sort of like a snow plow.

We finished with that operation and left for stand down around the end of January, and I had no idea where we were going until, to my surprise, our convoy of ten-ton trucks with the plows riding behind on the lowboy trailers, eventually pulled into my old 62nd Engineer Battalion motor pool in Long Binh. To my surprise, I was suddenly brought back into my old company area there, and quite fittingly, back to the very same bunk within the exact same hooch.

What are the chances of that happening?

To explain it: At that time, the 27th Land Clearing Team had then been reorganized as the 60th Land Clearing Company, and remnants of old and new were then combined into a more significant and complete force, with the 62nd Engineer Battalion converting itself by changing its designation from Construction to Land Clearing, in order to become a more inclusive support structure for its newly re-formed Land Clearing companies, which now were three in number, as there was the 60th, and the 501st (formerly the 86th Land Clearing Team), and a newly created one which drafted former key members of both former Land Clearing Teams to comprise much of its initial make-up, as it was called the 984th Land Clearing Company.

Upon arrival back at Long Binh Post, as I resumed my

old familiar pattern: I went straight on down to the EM Club, got drunk, and got into a fight. Platoon Sergeant Kirkpatrick had it in for me afterward. He said, "you will not be making the E-5 board".

From the start, I had made rank fairly quickly; oddly, even while considering my past incidences of disobedience. As it was, I was barred from reenlistment, but I kept getting promotions. Go figure. But I had grown to love my job as a plow operator, and being a bona fide 'Jungle Eater', even though it entailed long hours and hard, dirty work. Although strangely to some, I had found it to be the best duty I had been assigned to, with the best group of brothers to go along with it.

We didn't shave every day when out on our field operations, and didn't get bothered about it much by our superiors either, as they were mainly interested in the job at hand. Because of the warm humid weather, many of us had cut off our jungle fatigue pant legs, ripped the sleeves off our shirt, to gain some relief, while rarely bathing daily or even weekly, for that matter. Oftentimes, just a simple splash bath from a water-filled steel pot helmet seemed to be enough to wash away the grit and heavy dust on our faces and upper body areas from each day's activities, without having to take a full-on cold shower.

We regularly headed out to the cut early each morning at the appointed time, crawling our tractors in a single-file line; and at the end of the day we were always back at the NDP by dark. Then, maintenance on our equipment was called for, as we blew out the air breathers on the dozers and sharpened the blade and stinger while using the diesel-powered air compressor for those tasks, as the fuel truck would then come around and hand us the fuel nozzle to fill our tanks up again with diesel. Then, we were allowed to break away to enjoy our chow time before returning to the NDP motor pool for some further night maintenance, prior to being allowed to take a shower, or not, and then get some well-deserved sleep. It was at that time also when some of the guys would be able to take a few moments to write a letter or two to loved ones back home.

Rome Plows dragging a ship's anchor chain

Cutting small trees

There were a number of equipment mechanics assigned to each team or squad of plows, who were quick to perform any necessary repairs whenever needed. As operators, we had gotten involved in dropping belly pans on a regular basis to clear them of accumulative jungle debris that the heat from the engine and transmission would dry out quickly and create an on-going hazard of possibly sparking a belly pan fire, which was often difficult to put out because of where it was located, way up underneath the tractor; while one's limitations within a cramped space under the dozer had made their frantic attempts at extinguishing it all the more awkward. The more involved stuff, like replacing turbochargers, cracked heads, blown tracks, damaged radiators, etc., was completed by the dedicated maintenance teams who often worked all night to get as many of the plows as possible ready to go out to the 'cut' the following day.

In addition, our skilled welders would come around and re-weld any of the steel straps and screens on the cabs, as needed, or to sometimes even add a welded-on patch where the curved section of the blade may have been penetrated by some unforgiving object in the cut, or perhaps even from an explosive encounter with a land mine. These men were there to help hold the steel outer structure of these machines together for us with their artful welding skills, as best as possible, while falling trees and other hazards impacting on the tractor from time to time had caused some of the steel parts to break away from their previous welds.

Funny thing, I don't really know how I was able to actually do all that I had done in completing my tasks each day, with all that we had to do toward maintaining the equipment at night, as well as when working the trace during the morning and afternoon hours while staying alert to focus on cutting down the jungle. I like to think that much of it was probably attributed to just good old Southern ingenuity and grit.

Because of more involved cooperation with our mechanics and particular maintenance problems that were encountered, it sometimes even took me into the early morning hours before the work was finally completed. Then, almost like the blink of an eye, we were all back up at the crack of dawn to do it all over again.

During the hot season, it seemed that no one except us operators had fully realized that the temperatures in our cabs had often approached 140 degrees. A considerable amount of that heat was actually generated from the engine, up in front of the open-face cab, as it would naturally drift back into where the operator sat, while mixing with the already warm heat of the day to make it feel more like the operator was sitting in an oven. But we somehow weathered it and learned how to live with that hellish discomfort. To help matters, some of us oftentimes used a rag soaked with water from one's canteen and wrapped it around our necks to help cool us down a bit as we moved forward with the activities of the day.

For protection from land mines and other hazards as we operated these oddly configured contraptions, we sometimes wore a flak jacket and steel helmet, which would just add to the discomfort factor as we slow-cooked inside of those heat trapping cabs, even though we had steel screens on both sides and on the rear of the cab to help in venting much of the hot air. On the hotter days, the steel cabs got so scorching hot that we had to learn how to carefully enter and exit the tractors without grabbing onto any of the steel structure when climbing up or down, in order to keep from actually burning one's hands. Again, the use of a rag in one's hand tended to help overcome that problem, as we never were issued gloves to wear, to my recollection.

From a plow operator's perspective, it was often somewhat of a perplexing challenge to remember much about where we were on each operation, as we just went wherever they took us. Although, I think it might have been nice to at least have been privy to some general information about our whereabouts. Getting dropped off in the jungle by the 10-ton lowboys was a beginning. Getting retrieved by those same trucks six weeks later marked the conclusion of an operation. Without knowing very much about the particular geographic areas we were in; our various locations were not altogether notable as landmarks with names...at least to us. But for our leadership, who had maps and radios, they knew exactly where we were, and where we were going. Never, it seems, was this old saying or idiom truer for those times: *"It is not for us to wonder why, but simply to do or die."* As the Lowboy convoy returned to pick us up again, we were then transported back to the 62nd motor pool in Long Binh for two weeks of standdown, in order to re-tool and replace parts on our equipment before heading right back out on another operation.

Standdown, in addition to being the pause between cuts where the operators had to perform most of the basic maintenance on their dozers, was also the time when some of the tractors could be disassembled for significant repairs and parts replacement by our mechanics, as we were required to stand by and assist with things on these occasions, when called on. Things like replacing an entire engine, or one of the dozer's tracks, or pulling and replacing a damaged cab, etc. By the end of a six-week operation, we probably had 4 to 6 Rome Plows inoperable, or otherwise termed as 'Dead-lined', due to various causes.

As we readied for our next outing, I just prayed to God that He would deliver me through another operation. The first operation I was in was pretty uneventful. The second, as I recall, we had encountered many landmines and booby traps. It didn't take me long to spot those. My eyesight was just fine, as I could keenly spot a green trip wire stretched across my path within a green jungle.

I learned to heat my C-rations (Canned food rations) by using a small amount of C-4, which was a flexible and moldable, putty-like plastic explosive material. *In fact, it was featured in the movie, Caddy Shack, where Bill Murray had molded an amount of it into the form of a gopher.* But by itself without a detonator or blasting cap it is rendered inert, although it can safely be used for other purposes, like cooking, as it burns a lot like *Sterno*, and was found to be quite useful in quickly heating up our canned Army rations. It burned blue/green and was reasonably safe as long as you didn't hit it while it was lit.

Given that C-4 was a versatile type substance, we sometimes packed a four-ounce can with it to blow a hole in the ground, which was mostly comprised of laterite that was almost as hard as concrete in the dry season and became a muddy mess during Monsoon season. We also used C-4, more specifically, to fell giant trees, by attaching an amount of it to the trunk with a detonator, as it was quite effective in bringing down those trees that were too large and dangerous for the plow operators to tackle on their own with their blade stingers.

As some of us got tired of eating the same old thing all the time with these common C-rations, we found that they could occasionally be traded based on popularity. Even some members of our mechanized security were occasionally interested in trading their freeze-dried LRP (Long Range Patrol) rations for our C-rations. The LRP rations came in pouches, and had to be steeped in hot water before consuming the contents right out of the pouch, much like the freeze-dried varieties of entrees that people use nowadays when on camping trips. Such popular canned C-rations as Beenie weenies, spaghetti, beef stew, and pound cake were top favorites with a lot of the guys, having good trade value. But for entrees like scrambled eggs and ham, which had little trade value, it looked like the contents within had been chewed first by someone and then put back into the can.

These formerly WWII and Korean War canned food rations also had a Sundry pack pouch included, with a 5-pack of cigarettes and a packet of matches in it, along with a chocolate bar, a small roll of toilet paper, some saltine crackers, and sometimes even a small peanut butter cup, plus a packet of instant coffee, along with a powdered creamer. The chocolate was always found to be old and hard as a brick, with a strange white residue showing around it. But despite that, it did taste like chocolate. We generally ate that ration cold or heated it up a bit over C-4 to soften it.

Regular hot chow was prepared in the mess truck on Sundays and Holidays; or on other occasions, garbage cans were filled with water and a kerosene fired heater with a submersible arm was inserted, where all of the canned food would then be placed into the hot water to allow us to enjoy a hot dinner, or at least our own compromised version of it. We would just pluck out the heated cans with tongs and open them up with our trusty P-38 can openers.

Sometimes, like at Thanksgiving, hot chow that was the 'real deal', like turkey and the trimmings, or other holiday favorites, was sent out to us after being prepared in the company mess hall back at Long Binh, as it was flown out on a chopper with the mail, while being entirely contained in large sealed *Mermite* insulated cans to keep it hot. Those simple traditional offerings had served to raise our morale a bit, while helping to bring our overall awareness back to the spirit of the holidays, as we paused and enjoyed that evening meal, before heading back over to our NDP motor pool for some further night maintenance.

Among our company's basic arsenal of weapons, we had M-79 grenade launchers, shotguns, and .45 caliber pistols. Most of the operators carried an M-3 grease gun in .45 caliber. The stock on it was retractable, so it easily fit within the cramped space inside the Rome Plow's cab. Later, we were all issued the M-14 rifle, made by Springfield Arms, of which many of us had trained with during Basic Training, and knew it to be reliable and accurate in delivering .308 caliber (or 7.62 Nato) firepower. Although, it was heavier than most rifles, and was found to be rather difficult to secure inside of the tractor's cab. They were also among the surplus leftovers from WWII and Korea.

At one point, when we were on an operation during March of 1969, where we lost twenty-seven Rome Plows to mines and maintenance issues in only about three days of activity, it effectively brought things to a complete standstill for us, having resulted in A-Company being called on to come back out to pick us all up with their 10-ton lowboys, as the operation was temporarily terminated, or paused. We then spent the next two weeks putting the Plows back into good working condition before heading directly back out to where we were before, and picked up right where we left off.

Chinook helicopters had often delivered numerous items to our field locations during these lengthy land clearing operations, to regularly include the transport of water while routinely towing two 600-gallon black rubber bladders of it out to our locations, as needed. One was potable, while the other was non-potable.

For much of the next thirty days on that operation, we were pounded with mortars and rockets at breakfast, and also while out in the cut, and sometimes even at supper time, during that intense period of enemy activity. Because of that constant barrage of incoming ordinance, we were unable to get water delivered by the Chinook helicopters for some time, as we then had to resort to rationing the water we had. Because of that, another soldier and I sometimes had to guard the water purifier and its related equipment.

While on this occasion I don't recall our exact location at the time, I do remember that it was Mother's Day, 1969. It was nearly dusk and I was under the shower bucket when mortars were suddenly flying straight at our row of tents. I immediately ran to my tent to get my rifle, and as I did, a mortar landed on the tent next to mine. Jerry Ninko and I then ran to the bunker that I had chipped into the side of the trench wall where we had pitched tents during the dry season. There were four guys already packed in it.

were both hit by shrapnel, but nothing seri-
tent that was hit was where Mike Pinksaw
as hit and evacuated. Years later, at the first
reunion I attended at Ft. Leonard Wood, I discovered that
the medic triage on that operation wanted to leave Mike
behind because his injuries appeared fatal to them. Sergeant Dave Minto, it was reported, then pulled a pistol on
the dust-off helicopter pilot and ordered him to load Mike.
I spent years wondering and not knowing that Mike was
actually still alive, having fully recovered from his nearly
fatal wounds.

*At this writing, Mike Pinksaw was known to be still alive
and well, living in the state of Rhode Island.*

At that time, when I was dusted off (*transported by helicopter to a field hospital*), after being seen and determined to
be okay, I spent the night in the hospital and was sent back
to the company in the nude; but a buddy thankfully gave
me a large shirt to help cover up. The overall attitude was
that it was just another day in our lives, and we had an important job to do.

But, to backtrack a bit, I had observed a very tragic and
shocking scene when being dusted off late that day, as I
was carried out by a stretcher to the chopper for transport-
ing to a field hospital. From my stretcher, I noticed them
picking up an infantry soldier whose left arm was partially
detatched. Along the way, as we came closer, I could see
that parts of his chest and face were also missing.

Writing this has dug up many unsettling memories.
This old memory of Mike Pinksaw had haunted me for
nearly 45 years. Like many survivors, I sometimes ask myself, "why am I still here when so many other young men
paid the ultimate price?"

Other memories from being in the jungle:

When pulling water from a green swamp, we had about 300-rounds of ammo and a few grenades between the three of us, as we had been assigned on a detail to collect non-potable water for our equipment and whatever else we might use it for, except not to drink it. The experience of that detail and being a Rome Plow Operator constantly exposed us to an enemy we could not see, sometimes seemingly lurking within only a few yards of us. We were a pretty open target at times. As a result of our Land Clearing accomplishments and how the cleared areas were affecting movements where enemy supply routes were involved, it was later reported or rumored to us that there was an actual cash bounty put out on our heads by our adversarial foes within Ho Chi Minh's Communist government to the north, at $2,500 to kill a plow operator and $5,000 to disable the tractor. We regularly kept plenty of pot around and, when we could get it, a pint of Old No. 7 to boot.

I believe God protects children, idiots, and drunks. At any given time, I was all three. But the lesson here is that not everyone comes home from war intact; at least not entirely. Many of us who did come home are forever haunted by our wartime experiences.

But, through it all, I can proudly say this in total sincerity: If I were to ever find myself in a war again, I could do no better than when I served with the men of the 27th/60th Land Clearing Company: the *'Jungle Eaters'.* A better bunch of crazies there will never be.

If you have not done so already, consider visiting the Vietnam War Memorial in Washington, DC.

CPT William T. "Tom" Frantz

HHC, 62nd Engineer Battalion
&
984th Land Clearing Company
1970 – 1971
Company Commander
Hometown: Sanford, North Carolina

A Day in the Jungle

This story is dedicated to the Engineers who manned the Land Clearing teams, companies and battalions. Their contribution, although not highly documented, was as significant as any unit serving in Vietnam.

The Vietnam War followed the same pattern as other recorded wars. Most of the stories are told about the classic combat arms of infantry, artillery and cavalry, but current writers have added armor, air cavalry and tactical air. These areas are written about because of the interesting battles and tactics. This particular story is about one of the toughest units in Vietnam – the 984th Engineer Land Clearing Company. It was our job to reduce enemy strongholds, like the Iron Triangle and HoBo and Bo Loi Woods, to pastures, which would take away one of the enemy's most powerful weapons – concealment. I was the company commander, and it was my job to make sure we achieved our mission and that I sent all of my troops home alive.

The land-clearing companies had three different types of missions: To open lines of communications by clearing major highways so that U.S. and ARVN units could be supplied by land. To cut around major bases in providing fields of fire to limit the enemy's ability to approach undetected, and to eliminate enemy bases reportedly within the areas cut.

Execution and Organization

Each Land Clearing company was sent out into locations where an armored cavalry squadron or a mechanized infantry battalion met with them, from within their divisional area of operations, to coordinate efforts on supporting a land clearing mission. These mechanized units provided security for the cuts and the overall security for the night defensive positions (NDP's). The normal setup was for the land clearing company to work their 'cut' in close cooperation with a cavalry troop or mechanized infantry company.

The engineer commander was responsible for clearing a given area while the security commander tried to give them enough room to work in, as both of them maintained cooperation via radio communication. The goal was to clear 100 to 200 acres of medium to triple canopy jungle each day for 45 days. A given mission would effectively clear 4,000 to 8,000 acres of jungle.

From the bottom up, the land clearing battalions were designed to support the Rome plow, which was the heralded piece of specially designed heavy equipment that was chosen for the task of clearing heavy foliage and triple canopy jungle in many of the trouble-spot areas of South Vietnam.

These plows were specially modified Caterpillar D7E and D9 dozer type crawler tractors. Each plow had a special blade designed to cut trees several inches from the ground. The blade had a sharpened lower edge and a knockdown bar at the top that pushed trees and cut debris forward and to the right. By properly using the track clutches, an operator could run several feet of the blade across a tree to easily cut it down. If the tree was too big, he could split the tree with a built-in elongated steel wedge, called a 'stinger', that protruded forward from the left edge of the blade. The stinger was a piece of solid hardened steel about a foot long, three inches wide and six inches tall, built into the left side of the blade. Both the stinger and the blade were sharpened every night in the NDP motor pool to maintain the effectiveness of the blade. The plow also had a reinforced steel cab to protect the operator from falling branches and trees.

By 1970, some of the D7 and all four of the D9's had water tanks mounted on the roofs of these cabs. The water tanks, with the use of a connected hose, allowed operators to more easily extinguish belly pan fires. The cabs also had metal protective guards mounted above all of the vulnerable hydraulic lines.

Most of the Land Clearing companies had about 30 of these plows and were doing a great job to get at least 24 of them out to the cut in the mornings. There was always a lot of competition between the individual operators to see how many days in a row they could make it into the cut. Each platoon had 10 plows, nine with cutting blades and one with a normal flat "bull" blade. Each company had three cutting platoons and a maintenance platoon.

The battalion itself had three land-clearing companies, a maintenance/transportation company and a headquarters company.

Coordination and Control:

Each day, we were expected to clear 100 to 200 acres of jungle. The thicker the jungle the less got cleared. Each evening, I would meet with the security company commander to discuss the next day's cut. This covered how the units would get to the area to be cut, how the morning cut would be laid out and secured, and where the afternoon cut would probably be. The afternoon plans became much clearer during the lunch break the next day. Afterwards, security personnel could determine where the on-call artillery concentrations for the next day would be located.

I controlled the operation from a light observation helicopter (LOH). While the units were getting ready, I would go up and scout the area to ensure there were no obvious surprises. When the cut started, I would guide the lead plow from the air via radio contact in order to get the size and shape of the cut correct and protect the lead plow from being ambushed or from falling into streams, bomb craters and ravines. During enemy contact, the control of the companies went over to the security commander. If the jungle was not too thick, the trees were fairly small, and there was no enemy on the flanks, a very effective tactic when sighting the enemy in the 'cut', was to have a platoon of plows charge forward with the security armored calvary assault vehicles (ACAVs) moving right behind them. Although they were not completely armored vehicles, it was pretty hard for the enemy to stand their ground with these plows coming on at walking speed and pushing down trees like 60-foot fly swatters.

Just like most of the other soldiers in the field, the plow operators woke up stiff. When it gets over 100 degrees every afternoon and the temperature in the dozer cab gets up to 120 degrees or more, a mere 63 degrees overnight seemed like freezing. The normal wake-up call at 5:00 a.m. was from the roar of a dozer starting up, just 10 yards away. A 400-horsepower engine starting up tended to wake most operators, but some were so exhausted they actually had to be shaken. Sharpening blades kept operators up until 10:00 or 11:00 at night, and mortar attacks had often interrupted and ate into one's sleep once it came. It was not entirely unusual for operators to get by on three or four hours of sleep a night.

Wake-up calls sent by the Vietcong and North Vietnamese were far louder and less pleasant, and many operators resorted to sleeping under their dozers in the event of night attacks. Being under the transmission of the D7 was one of the safest places during a mortar or rocket attack. In this position operators had the cab, floorboards, engine and the transmission between them and any incoming artillery rounds.

Crawl-out, Maintenance and Layout:

Each morning the plows and mechanized security would gather up into platoons and then start the crawl out to that day's cut. Even though the area might be adjacent to the one from the previous day, a new road would have to be cut for the procession of plows and tanks, APC's, M548 maintenance track, and other related vehicles to travel on, in creating a safer path while heading out to engage again with the jungle.

As a unit commander, I never wanted to establish a pattern. We would get the whole area cut, but how we did it was always unpredictable. This effectively decreased the number of casualties due to ambushes, booby traps and mines.

Every day each plow was maintained at least four times. In the morning the operator checked the oil, hydraulic fluid, water and fuel levels, and rechecked his previous evenings work. From November to February the maintenance was really tough because most of it was done before it got light or after it got dark.

After the crawl out to the cut, and four or five hours of cutting, the operators took a break for lunch and maintenance. Each operator idled down the plow without turning it off, and then pulled another round of maintenance. During maintenance the M548 would come around to each plow and give the operator some ice water and add oil and hydraulic fluid if necessary.

After maintenance each operator ate his C rations and then either worked on other mechanical problems, talked to his buddies or fell fast asleep in the operator's seat. After the first week of the normal 45-day cut, given the daily requirements, most of the personnel were on the verge of exhaustion.

As it applied to Area Cuts, the idea of the layout was to create the outline of a large area that the plows would stay busy with, while continuing to clear it all out for the rest of the morning or afternoon. By doing this, plows could continue to clear toward the center when the helicopter had to leave to refuel. It also allowed for one of the bull blade dozers to build a road around the cut so the armored personnel carriers (APCs) could move around without destroying their suspensions, transmissions and radios. In the jungle, even lightly loaded track vehicles had problems while most of our security tracks had three times the basic load of ammo aboard. By the time the helicopter returned, it was nearly time again to create another initial outline.

All of the 548 maintenance tracks were heavily loaded with spare parts, extra water, oil and hydraulic fluid, to add with the welding unit that was already onboard. During the first circuit of the cut, the APCs were posted as security around the outside of the trace. Then, as the plows continued to cut the area out concentrically to reveal more open space, the security's APC's and tanks would then move in to follow the activity a little more closely and provide their reassuring presence.

The morning and afternoon cut layout was always the hardest time of the day due to enemy attacks. The security unit officer and I would fly around in the LOH looking for trouble that might be waiting. We would fly a hundred feet over the trees to draw fire and look for other problems such as bunkers, booby traps, ambushes, bomb craters, streams, swamps or ravines. Some of these potential hazards could kill, but others merely slowed us down.

Almost every day we had a certain number of plows that had just stopped in the cut. During one week I had to transport operators out by Med-Evac for two broken ankles, a centipede sting, multiple bee stings, snakebite, a tarantula bite, a scorpion sting, third-degree burns and heat prostration. My unit lost nine operators without a single enemy contact. All but the burned operator came back within a day or two on one of the Chinook supply helicopters.

Every day I reported to the Corps Commander on how many acres were cut. One of my reports actually became a part of history in VIETNAM STUDIES, U.S. Army Engineers, 1965-1970:

▸ of the intense command interest in land-clear-
ions, daily production reports received careful
scrutiny at all echelons. Unit commanders and even troops
themselves quickly learned this fact, and competition between land-clearing companies became intense.

*The most forthright production report ever received was sub-
mitted by a company commander whose Rome Plows had all become hopelessly mired in the monsoon mud before reaching the
cut area. His report for the day in the line reserved for "acres
cleared" was the most famous one-liner in land-clearing history.
It said, "one tree."*

*Needless to say, this report created great concern as it filtered
up through channels. An investigation clearly disclosed the impossible situation of the unit; in fact, to cut down a single tree
under the circumstances was a major achievement. Queried further on this point, the company commander admitted that one
of his plow operators had attached his winch cable to a dead tree
in an attempt to extract his tractor from the mud. As the winch
pulled on the cable the tree fell over and was counted.*

With up to twelve hours in the cut and three or four
more spent doing maintenance, it was very difficult for the
operators to stay clean each day, especially during Monsoon. Interestingly, many of them found that they had a
better chance of preventing jungle rot if they only bathed
every third day.

By the end of a 45-day cut, most of the operators and
mechanics were exhausted, and their jungle fatigues, for
all practical purposes, had mostly by then become oily,
sweaty, smelly rags. So, as a result, some of the men had
to be re-supplied with new Jungle fatigues more often than
some others.

I remember one time when the 984th returned to Long

Binh from a completed operation, the men off-loaded the tractors from all of the low-bed trailers, dropped the blades and headed for the main PX to buy soap, shaving gear and everything else we had been missing for the last six and a half weeks. In front of the PX my soldiers were stopped by two sergeants in starched jungle fatigues, and told they were too dirty to enter. I arrived right after my men and was nearly as dirty as they were. Seeing the situation, I stood the sergeants at attention, complete with salute, while my men walked into the PX to get what they needed.

Rank does have some privileges, and it was the least I could do for my troops. I salute these men, most of whom had volunteered to be in this elite unit, whose mission it was to clear the jungle and reduce the element of risk for other soldiers.

SP/5 Terry T. Brown

86th Engineer Battalion Land Clearing Team
&
501st Land Clearing Company
1968 - 1969
Rome Plow Operator & Squad Leader
Hometown: Walnut Creek, California

Stand-Downs

D uring 1968, when I was with the 86th Engineer Battalion's Land Clearing Team out in Bearcat basecamp, which was located roughly 10 or 12 miles southeast of Bien Hoa, along QL-15 highway in the Central Lowland region of South Vietnam, otherwise known as the III Corps Tactical Zone, we had all been kept busy after returning from a 45-day field operation, working daily out in our motor pool while making needed repairs and replacing parts on our tractors and other pieces of equipment. This was to go along with the regular maintenance that was commonly called for, in getting everything back up and fully operational again, before loading the plows back onto the low bed trailers and lining our vehicles up in convoy formation to head right back out again on another field operation of similar duration. This maintenance-focused interlude that occurred regularly between operations, was commonly referred to as a 'Stand-Down', which routinely served as a necessary 15-day break between our usual 45-day field operations.

In addition to re-tooling and restoring the mechanical workability on our equipment, the days of Stand-Down also gave us all ample time to enjoy some of the simple pleasures that we had missed when working in the field, like actually staying clean for a time by having hot showers readily available to us again, while wearing clean jungle fatigues for a change, and enjoying hot homey meals for breakfast, lunch and dinner-time in the mess hall again (instead of eating C-rations much of the time). Also, just having an opportunity to join with others occasionally for a few leisurely beers after hours at our Enlisted Men's Club had offered us another way to relax.

Another particular Stand-Down perk had afforded us the opportunity to gather at the battalion's makeshift outdoor movie theater at night, to take in a 'flick' while sucking down a few cans of beer and just allowing our minds to rest a bit, before having to head back out and spend another 45 days in the jungle, where we found that smiles and laughter were somewhat harder to come by.

Plus, just being able to get our built-up collection of dirty laundry washed and dried was something of an importance to us all, if not a priority during Stand-Down, even though we didn't actually accomplish it ourselves. For that, our friendly 'Hooch girls,' or billet-cleaning Vietnamese ladies, would oblige with that task, in taking our accumulation of laundry home with them, to wash it all at a nearby stream while laying the washed and rinsed items out on boulders to dry in the Sun, before they then folded and wrapped all of our clothes back up in brown paper, tied with twine, and returned these packages of our freshly laundered jungle fatigues and undergarments back to us, placed like gifts upon our bunks. For our part, the nominal fee for that service was always placed under our pillows where they were known to find it. We generally paid these gals with our military script, which was called, MPC, or Military Payment Certificates, and they would then have the given dollar amount exchanged somewhere off post into their own monetary form, which I believe was called 'Dong'. Occasionally, their payments for this service also came in the form of actual U.S. Dollars, whenever a few of the newer guys in the unit still had possession of some leftover greenbacks to spend.

Oftentimes, some of our freshly laundered jungle fatigues would come back to us with battery acid holes and permanent stains that wouldn't wash out, revealing more of the nature and degree of our involvement as land clearing engineers. So, it sometimes became necessary for some of us at that time to make a call on our supply sergeant to provide us with a re-issue of new fatigues.

But, also during these more tranquil times of renewal which Stand-Down had represented, we were immediately reminded (*or hounded*) by our First Sergeant about our outward appearance, as he demanded that we all shave regularly while back at the company area, and told us all to go and get haircuts. While we were in the field, nobody much cared about what we looked like, for the most part, so long as we did our jobs. However, when coming back to Bearcat, our arrival had apparently brought us all back to reality, with a sudden return to civilization, and our First Sergeant was always quite adamant while bringing that unwanted awareness back into our minds. This 15-day period of renewal had also allowed us time to go to the post PX, in order to get re-supplied with certain items and toiletries that we would tend to run short of in the field.

When on Standdown during the dry season there, as the days became annoyingly hot and humid, I would occasionally volunteer to go out to the rock quarry just outside of the post, while serving as 'shotgun' for one of the battalion's 5-ton dump truck drivers. They were occasionally called on to go out there to pick up a load of gravel or rock for a particular project; although my sole interest in going was to be able to go for a swim in the big pond that was out there, and enjoy its cooling effects, before jumping back into the cab of the truck, soaking wet, and heading back to the compound. The extreme heat of the day had then provided hot flows of air inside the truck, which had always dried me off quite fast. There was no such vehicle of any kind there at that time that might have been equipped with an air conditioning unit. So, we all just rolled with that punch and endured the intense heat and humidity as best as we could.

But, whenever one of those rare opportunities to cool off at the quarry arose, during a time when I wasn't needed at my plow, it represented a nice little getaway from the usual sweat producing activities occurring daily out in the hot and dusty motor pool.

Aside from having a PX market available to us there at this fairly small basecamp, there wasn't much else in the way of other available ammenities or services on post, except for a Vietnamese steambath and massage parlor, where the combination of those two theraputic treartments left us feeling quite fresh and renewed. While the steambath was just "what the doctor ordered", and had helped to open up one's pores and soften stiff muscles, the massage was altogether different than anything I might have expected, as it involved the use of these small young

Vietnamese lady's feet, as they would climb up on the massage table and walk all over our bodies while massaging the legs, buttocks, and back muscles with their toes and the heals of their feet. While it was quite strange and a little unnerving at first, we would soon get more accustomed to their lighter body weight as they continued to walk and massage until covering all of the areas of one's backside. When finished, and exiting their shop, we could immediately feel that it actually made a huge difference, with nearly euphoric feelings of renewal exhibited.

As our field operations tended to vary in terrain and types of foliage encountered, we continued to move around within the III Corps area of operations to take on other cutting assignments for the different Infantry divisions of the region. For the areas where we would initially set up our circular earthen berm, which was the defining outer perimeter that ringed around our night defensive positions where we worked on our equipment and ate and slept, the lay-out for it was done along the lines of how it was originally designed for practical useage. The overall dimensions for the encampment were generally in keeping with the need for enough space to accommodate all of the plows and maintenance vehicles, while providing adequate room for a motor pool area, as well as enough space for a mess area and unit personnel tents. Plus, the establishment of a 12 –15 foot deep garbage sump to dispose of our trash, which was always dug out with the use of a bull blade dozer when laying out the temporary compound's workable dimensions on the open landscape.

The various U.S. Infantry Divisions representing most of the given areas where we worked, had usually provided us with some of their own mechanized infantry units, in the form of heavily armed track vehicles, consisting of APC's and tanks, which contained a workable contingent of armed infantrymen, to effectively secure and watch-over us while we worked the 'Cut'; as it was entirely in their own best interest to protect those who would be im-proving on the divisional area's landscape, where they would benefit from our efforts by gaining greater visibility over any possible enemy activities or suspected move-ment.

That was how these LC missions worked, in a coordi-nated way, as the security unit was there to help keep the engineers reasonably safe from harm while everyone fo-cused on the task at hand as the mission progressed. Over the course of time, we had worked alongside numerous mechanized infantry companies, whose job it was to sur-round our NDP sites at night, while positioning their tanks and armored personnel carriers just inside of the circular berm, strategically placed to monitor and scan for possible insurgent activity out around the perimeter, while they would also surround and provide armed protection for our trace cutting locations out in the jungle during the day. Their needed presence, and their almost magical, yet pro-fessional level of attention in detecting possible enemy movement or aggression within those areas were com-monly well noted and appreciated, along with their quick and thorough responses to anything that might occur.

Whether it was when we worked in the AO within the Tropic Lightning's 25th Infantry Divisional sphere, or for the Big Red One's 1st Infantry Divisional area, or out in the Blackhorse area of the 11th Armored Cavalry Regi-ment's assigned territory, along with other notables in the III Corps zone, we were well looked after by these divisional mechanized units, while we performed our own particular magic by making the jungle disappear.... or at least getting it to go horizontal.

But, while remembering some of these mechanized protective forces that had helped to keep us all as safe as possible during our missions, one particular unit stood out for us during 1969, after the 86th Land Clearing Team had joined with the 62nd Engineer Battalion in Long Binh, to become the 501st Land Clearing company. With that new development for the unit, three Land Clearing companies were at that time created within a unique Engineer Battalion that was then set up to provide them with full maintenance support, unlike what the 86th LCT had available for that in Bearcat; especially after the 86th Battalion had followed the 9th Infantry Division, in moving out of Bearcat in mid-1968, to relocate within the IV Corps Tactical Zone's Delta region south of there, as they had effectively left us all on our own, to find our own means of support wherever we could. In effect, we had become orphaned. But, as the signature engineer battalion for the 9th Division, the 86th were clearly designated as a construction battalion, while we were a whole different classification as a company size unit, being uniquely designated as 'land clearing'. Although, while the 86th Engineer Battalion had always maintained a symbiotic relationship with us in Bearcat, that all suddenly changed when they were called on to rejoin with the 9th Infantry Division in Dong Tam.

But I digress.

Anyway, with regard to the particular mechanized security outfit that I was alluding to, we were somewhat surprised to see, on one field operation when I was with the 501st Land Clearers that an Australian mechanized unit was assigned to secure us, as we had never before encountered the likes of these guys.

They were members of the 3rd Australian Cavalry, and were found to be very focused and business-like when on the job of securing us, while also being outrageously fun-loving and downright comical whenever they had some free time to gather with some of us at night in the NDP. We had them securing us for about 10 or 12 days on that operation, as I recall, before another U.S. security team came in to relieve them. Although, when we awoke on the morning when the new security team arrived, we found that the Aussies had previously departed. But quite unbeknown to us, our friends from down-under had quietly left us with tiny souvenirs, as they had quietly stenciled the image of a little kangaroo on the side of each of our plows with white paint, serving as little mementos to remember them by.

* * *

Interestingly, one of those Australian Troopers, named Les Dunstan, who was from the state of Queensland, Australia, in a suburb near Brisbane, had developed a strong friendship with a few of our guys from the 501st, while having maintained telephone and letter contact with them over the years since; and when the former 86th & 501st Land Clearing Engineers had hosted a reunion some years later in West Virginia, Les was invited to come. Given the overall distance, geographically, it seemed entirely unlikely. But he surprised everyone by actually coming all that way from Queensland to attend the reunion and hang out with guys that he hadn't seen since that brief period of time when his unit was securing us in Vietnam, back in 1969. In seeing that, it seemed that nothing could have been more surreal.

In another particular remembrance related to those by-gone days in Vietnam, this one had to do with my friend and former plow operator, squad leader, and later platoon sergeant, Bob Watson, along with another friend and plow operator from my days with the 86th Land Clearing Team, former SP-4 John Sorrick, as they had both traveled with me from our 2010 reunion location in Branson, MO, while driving some 90 miles northeast of there to Fort Leonard Wood, on a side trip, in order to visit the Army's Engineer Museum.

Upon arrival, and just prior to entering the museum, we walked around the grassy grounds there, to check out the variety of outdated vehicles that had been placed all around so that visitors could appreciate the various types of armored track vehicles, trucks, and other assorted pieces of heavy equipment displayed that were commonly used during the U.S. Army's previous involvements in the wars and conflicts of the 20th century. It was plain to see that this notable old assemblage of vehicles and various types of equipment was purposely placed there to serve in highlighting the entryway to the museum building.

Among all of these relics collectively positioned there, we then came upon a fully restored D7E Rome Plow trac-tor, as the three of us just suddenly paused, while standing there marveling at the familiar sight of it. Intently moving around it while climbing onto its tracks to look into the cab, Watson then stepped back down with tears streaming down his cheeks, as he was suddenly overcome with emo-tions, while unexpectedly coming back into full visual and physical contact again with the mechanical icon that best represented his service in the Vietnam war.

Sadly, Bob is gone now, as he passed-on in December of 2021 at his home in Fort Morgan, Colorado. But, for that brief moment back in 2010, three former unit mates stood by together to reminisce, and to appreciate our own involvements with each other, when laboring with our Land Clearing operations in South Vietnam, some years ago, during 1968 and 1969.

If you have not traveled to Fort Leonard Wood, in the Springfield area of southern Missouri, to visit the Army's Engineer Museum there, you might think about adding it to your bucket list of things yet to do. Granted, it is nothing like sky diving or running with the Bulls; but if you are any kind of a history buff, you should find it nothing short of fascinating, as the Army's storied Corps of Engineers have been in existence since the time of the Revolutionary war.

Motor Pool at Bearcat

NDP Field Motor Pool

Windrowing near Xuan Loc, 1968

A Rome Plow with the 86th Land Clearing Team operating south of Long Binh, South Vietnam, July 1968. (U.S. Army Corps of Engineers).

Big John Sorrick, Terry Brown, and Bob Watson at Fort Leonard Wood in 2010

SP/5 Daniel Gonzalez

59th Land Clearing Company, 39th Engineer Battalion
Company Medic
1970 – 1971
Hometown: Unknown

* This detailed account was actually written in March of
1971, when SP-5 Gonzalez was still in-country.

*SP5 Daniel Gonzalez served as a combat medic with the 59th
Engineer Company (Land Clearing), 39th Engineer Battalion.
During 1970-71 he served side by side with soldiers of the 1st
Battalion, 6th Infantry during land clearing operations in the
Batangan Peninsula, in the vicinity of Hill 43, Hill 128, Hill 76,
and Hill 109.*

A Medic's View

I have been in Vietnam for a little over a year now, and
looking back over the past twelve months, many
things come to mind. Vietnam is a tragic land, both to
the indigenous inhabitants, and to the American Servicemen. Yet, strangely enough, it is also a land of breath-tak-
ing beauty. The one flaw to this beauty has to do with the
constant danger to one's life that exists in the form of the
Viet Cong guerrillas, the North Vietnamese Army Regu-
lars, and perhaps more significantly for my unit, booby-
traps and land mines. I don't mean to infer that the former
hasn't been an imminent threat to GIs throughout Vietnam,

but speaking from my experience with the 59th Engineer Company (Land Clearing), the majority of our misfortunes have been a direct result of the latter.

Arriving in Phou-Bai, within the Northern Highland region of South Vietnam, also referred to as the I Corps Tactical Zone of operations, I was told I would be placed in a Land Clearing Unit, and that I wouldn't have it bad at all. As it turned out, I was pretty lucky, in that I was one of four medics in the company, and needless to say, was the "*cruit*" among them. This is quite significant to me, because these guys taught me to have confidence in myself and were always nearby whenever I had a question pertaining to my job. To be completely honest, I was scared (*although that doesn't completely describe my feelings*), as I knew that I was inexperienced as a medic, although fully trained for the task. But my peers had assured me that when the time came to prove myself, I would be there doing what had to be done.

Before moving to Chu Lai, we were working a cut in an area northwest of Quang Tri (*near the village of Mai Loc*). While in this area, most of my patient's maladies consisted of minor burns, cuts, colds, and the common illnesses of mankind. But the majority of them were due to the direct results of enemy action.

In July of 1970 we arrived in Chu Lai. Little did any of us realize at the time how many of our men would be hurt in the coming days. Numerous rumors had circulated throughout the company that our new target area of operations was heavily mined, and these rumors proved to be true. A group of us remained in Chu Lai, while one platoon was still up north finishing a job, and the remaining core of the company: two platoons of Rome Plow operators, maintenance and communications personnel, had gone on to the Batangan Peninsula.

The very first day out in the field, we had a medevac occur when one of our dozer operators hit a booby-trap, as he was transported directly to the Army hospital in Chu Lai for surgery and recovery. At the time, because my unit had others there in recovery from their wounds, I had to stay in Chu Lai for a month before going back out to the field. While there I set up, as best I could, a sick ward for our men who were released from the hospital. My job was to care for them further, until they were ready to return to duty, and to provide the medics in the field with additional medical supplies. Every day, I awoke with the same question on my mind, "Who will be hurt today?" And every day for weeks at a time, someone would be medevac'd due to shrapnel inflicted by land mines, booby-traps, or some other VC invention.

In another tragic incident, one man died (as a non-hostile casualty) when the dozer he was operating rolled over and plummeted down the side of a hill.

Doc Thomas, another medic, had rushed to him and even boarded the med-evac chopper, giving mouth-to-mouth resuscitation; but when the chopper reached the 91st Evac Hospital, he was dead on arrival. This incident was a heavy cross for the members of our unit to bear, for we had lost a real friend. They say death is a blessing, but that doesn't keep us from asking or wondering why.

Right after this incident, I went back out to the field. One particular day, just before noon, another operator hit a booby-trap. To again go out on the cut and sit on the M548 maintenance track and watch the dozers clear the land isn't very interesting after you've seen them do it day in and day out, week after week. However, one thing is always present in my mind, and that is the fear that one of my buddies will get hurt and possibly die at any time during these operations. These were the thoughts going through my mind when I suddenly heard an explosion off in the distance. It is a terrible, empty, weak, and sickening feeling when an explosion goes off and you know someone is hurt.

The M548 was situated some distance away from the casualty in this case, and when getting over there it could only manage to maneuver in so far, to get somewhat close to the victim due to the steep terrain. Before I actually realized what I was doing, I immediately jumped off the M548 track and rushed over to the casualty. After he was medevac'd, I realized that the experience had been just as my peers had said, "One acts without realizing it".

Every day since arriving in Viet Nam, I've started out with a silent prayer to God asking for his help and protection for all of the men in our unit. The 'Cut', as the daily operation of clearing is called, begins at around 8:00 a.m. when we leave the NDP. The dozers lead the way, followed by the APCs with armed infantrymen onboard, and a Sheridan tank for added security. Then comes the M548 track, carrying the Commanding officer or Platoon leader, the NCOIC, the demolition personnel, and a medic.

The cut is set up by the lead dozer, which in this case the operator maintains radio communications via a helmet headset with the officer in the M548 as the plows begin to tear down shrubs, trees, and whatever else that may stand in the area to be cleared. The M548 then stations itself so that its occupants can see all or most of the dozers as they worked the trace. This way, much of their progress can be monitored, while making it easier to locate a dozer in the event of an accident or injury, or a breakdown that will involve assistance from the mechanics onboard.

As if the hidden dangers weren't enough, the changing topography had often presented numerous problems, especially in muddy areas and rocky terrain. Occasionally in steeper areas, a dozer will roll or turn over on its side causing injuries to the operator. So, after expecting the worst from this sort of accident, and then finding the operator with only a scratch or two, everyone tends to let out a sigh of relief before the jokes and playful jabs begin. Finally, the task of setting the dozer up-right is tackled and the operator is soon back on his way.

Numerous tunnels have often been found during these operations. Here is where the demo man earns his keep. Once he checks it out for enemy supplies or ammunition, he then blows the tunnel with a charge of C-4 plastic explosives. On numerous occasions, we have found caches of food (rice and corn), articles of clothing, ammo, and various types of enemy rifles, etc.

At chow time, everyone comes together to talk about a million and one things. During this time the soda girls or *soda dollies* as they are also called, make their appearance if they haven't already done so by now, and the old familiar tones of 'song and dance' are heard: "*You buy soda from me?*" For some strange reason the girls think that an American GI's stomach is bottomless; for, no sooner do you drink your soda down, then the girls are on you again, "*Why you no buy soda from me? You buy soda from her.*" Although, why we had actually paid fifty cents per each soda is still beyond me, when we can get them from the company for fifteen cents. But then, the girls' sodas are cold, and the girls are quite cute, and it's no secret that a young woman's charm is a man's handicap.

The work continues out in the cut each day until four o'clock comes around, and then we start the procession back to the NDP. The operators then pull maintenance and another day is done; but only for the same process to repeat itself again in the following days until the operation has finally been completed, to where the men and equipment are then all convoyed back to our main base camp for a 15-day maintenance standdown, before heading back out to another operation…somewhere else.

SP/5 Thomas L. Randle Jr

60th Engineer Company (Land Clearing)
1969 – 1970
Wrecker Operator
Hometown: Clayton, Georgia

The Wrecker

Jumbo shrimp, rap music, and airplane food. What do they have in common? Military intelligence is another oxymoron. Seriously, the United States Army spent a small fortune training me to be a Construction Machine Operator, MOS 62E20, at Fort Leonard Wood (FLW), Missouri, also known as the ass hole of the United States. In fairness, wherever you attended basic training and AIT was known to you as the ass hole of the United States. MOS 62E20 is a typical job-related MOS amongst Rome Plow operators, but that was years away.

The honey hole at FLW is infamous and still in use. I visited FLW a few years ago and got an engineer school tour. Dear Lord! The engineer school was not only co-ed, but the commanding Lt. Col. was female, as was the battalion Sgt. Major. I went through the school from June-July, 1967. It was warm in Missouri in the summer. We operated Caterpillar D-7 tractors, Caterpillar 12 motor graders, and Caterpillar scrapers, poured some concrete and even laid some asphalt.

Now the men and women of the Engineers are operating Allis Chalmer tractors with air-conditioned cabs and steered by joysticks. Joy sticks? WTF? The joysticks are a nod to a generation that has played too many games, not enough time outdoors, and cannot be bothered to operate a tractor weighing over 31,000 pounds by levers. I spoke with a Master Sergeant who had 17 years in this man's Army. He was wearing suede boots and a camouflage uniform. He laughed and admitted that shining boots and polishing brass taught personal accountability and life skills.

To provide context to this story, I joined the Army in March 1967. I turned seventeen on February 13, and my sixteen-year-old girlfriend was pregnant. For us to be married, I needed my mother's signature to do so. She agreed if I joined the Army, which she had to authorize. With a 28-day delayed entry program, we were married on March 11, my wife turned 17 on March 17, and I reported to the induction center at NAS Jacksonville in April 1967. Six foot two, 147 pounds with ears so big I had to avoid being caught in a strong wind for fear I may levitate.

Basic training was at Fort Benning, Georgia, Harmony Church barrack, and Fort Leonard Wood (FLW), Missouri, in June 1967 for construction machine operator school. By the end of July 1967, I had completed that training and headed home for a 30-day leave.

I had a new wife and a daughter on the way. She was born on October 14, 1967. A perfect little girl then and now. I was a volunteer vs. a draftee and was permitted to choose my training and duty station. I selected Fort Stewart, Georgia, because it was the nearest Army fort to Jacksonville, Florida, my home.

I reported for duty in late August 1967. I was told there were no openings for construction machine operators and to report to the mess hall for training as a cook. WTF? A cook! They just invested thousands of dollars in training me to operate heavy equipment, and now they order me to become a cook. Has the Army lost its freaking mind?

I was not fond of it. But the positive that came from that was from a 'lifer' that took me under his wing and gave me some good advice on life. He assigned me a temporary duty station (TDY) to Hunter Army Airfield in Savannah, Georgia, which was easy duty. I was learning to prepare breakfast for hundreds of men and was exempt from bullshit like guard duty and KP. It was while at Hunter Army Airfield that my daughter was born.

I get a call from her stepfather telling me to come to Jacksonville Beach as my wife is going into labor. I requested a 3-day pass from a cranky old Staff Sergeant, who informed me, "If the Army wanted you to have a baby, they would have issued you one. You may have put that baby in her, but you cannot help pull it out. Leave denied." I called her stepfather back to say I could not come. He, unbeknown to me, called my company commander, whom I had never spoken with, or knew his name since I was TDY. He, in turn, called my Staff Sergeant and approved a 3-day leave. That went over the Sergeant's head and did not make him happy.

Shortly after, I was ordered to Germany, the 8th Army in Dexheim. By then, I had been promoted to SP/4 (E4), but with that damn cook designation in my 201 files. Again, I was fortunate to meet a Sgt. First Class from Arkansas, and when I explained that I hated being a cook, he helped. First, he assigned me to the Officer's Club as a short order cook, and he went with me into the village and obtained an apartment so that I could bring my wife and daughter to Germany. My daughter celebrated her first birthday in Germany.

I thought I would be in Germany for the 22 remaining months of my enlistment. We didn't have a car, so I often jogged to the base, about 2 kilometers. My family was there with me, and soon I was promoted to SP/5 (E5). Then the shit hit the fan.

While working as a short order cook in the Officer's Club, my primary duties were cooking burgers and making ice cream sundaes for the single officers. On this occasion, Sgt. First Class Pleasants of Arkansas came up the hill to the Officer's Mess and said a formal dinner was to be held. He would prepare the food and needed me to set up the dining room.

I broke out the white table cloths, good China, silverware, and glasses. Nearly took a chalk line to the tables and settings. It was friggin' perfect. That is until a woman burst through the swinging doors in the kitchen where I was enjoying myself. She began to upbraid me and said the dining room looked like an enlisted man's mess, blah, blah, blah. I did not possess the ability to stay quiet. She was the Battalion Commanders' wife. So, my smart-ass 18-year-old self says, "Who in the hell is the boss of this Battalion, you or your husband?"

To nobody's surprise, except my own, about 30 minutes later, Lt. Col. Sullivan came to see me and explained a few things I had not comprehended before smarting off to his wife. I was punished by being assigned to the motor pool. I still wasn't operating heavy equipment, but I was out of the mess halls. That was all I ever wanted. It was like Brer Rabbit getting thrown into the briar patch.

Later, in Vietnam, the morning after a particularly bad

mortar and rocket attack, and an exchange of rifle fire, a helicopter landed in our night defensive position (NDP). Who steps off? Lt. Col. Sullivan. Spit polished boots, starched uniform, and gleaming golden oak leafs on his lapels. I don't know why he was there since he wasn't the commander of the 62nd Engineer Battalion or in my chain of command. He spots me and starts singing my praises to my company commander. He tells my CO I was the best cook in Dexheim. My CO says that's funny; Randle's file doesn't mention being a cook. That will be funnier in a minute.

Back in Germany life as a soldier became normal—alerts, exercises, deployments, etc. We were sent to guard a village when Russia invaded Czechoslovakia in August 1968. They issued us live ammo. It was like an episode of Andy Griffith and Barney.

My teen wife had to go on base to do the laundry. I was by then pulling guard duty like most enlisted men. I had been on duty the previous night, so I was sleeping in our off-base apartment. I was awoken by my wife sitting on the edge of the bed, crying. I said, "what's wrong?' she said; I saw your name on a set of orders posted in the orderly room, and you are headed to Vietnam. Remember my encounter with the Lt. Col and his wife? It's no coincidence that as my 19th birthday approached, he ordered me to Vietnam.

I borrowed money to fly my wife and one-year-old daughter back to Jacksonville, and I spent a month or so by myself. I tried to use that time to see as much of Germany as possible. I then had 30-days' leave before reporting to Fort Dix for jungle training and deployment to Vietnam. We sat in dark theaters and watched movies about poisonous insects and snakes; how to identify them, and how not to contract the clap or gonorrhea. That was a joke, as the entire base was covered by snow, and the mock-up villages were buried under it.

I arrived in Vietnam in February 1969, and my 19th birthday was February 13. The 60th Land Clearing Company was to become my unit. They had been renamed from the 27th Land Clearing Company, formerly as a Team, about 30 days before my arrival. Almost all the men were part of the 27th's proud history.

Some more context here:

Nearly two years had passed since my training at FLW. In those days, soldiers hand carried their personnel files, called 201. I had mine, and during the 30-days of leave I was granted, I altered my 201 files and took white-out to my records. I covered all references to being a cook, so only the Construction machine operator MOS was visible. At long last, I was going to be an operator.

Wearing my new SP/5 insignia, I was flown by helicopter to the jungle where the 60th was on an operation. I walked up to Chief Warrant Officer Jack Thomas and said I was here and ready to be assigned to a Rome Plow, a Caterpillar D7E with a special blade and cab. Mr. Thomas, all 280 pounds of him, with a black handlebar mustache, shaved head, and shirtless, turned to me and said, "SP/5 Randle, get your tall, skinny ass over to that 5-ton wrecker and read the manual under the seat. You are the wrecker operator for the 60th Land Clearing Company; our only one, and will be working with all teams and maintenance."

But, Mr. Thomas, I am a trained 62E20 Construction Machine Operator. I know nothing about operating a wrecker or vehicles with pneumatic tires. "That's tough titty. We need a wrecker operator, and by God, you are it." Thus, in my entire 2 years, 10 months, and 23 days of active duty, I never operated a Construction machine. I ran that wrecker for 12 months. Its use was necessary to pull out radiator cores from a damaged D7E, assist in replacing a track blown off by land mines, or to lift off the entire cab. I worked long hours as I was the only one assigned to it. I was also the one at the tail end of all convoys, eating the dust of 30 ten-ton lowboys hauling the Rome Plows to and from the assigned areas that were cut.

Sometimes, I stopped and used the hook to lift a trailer so that a flat tire could be changed. The convoy continued on, and it was uneasy being left behind on the side of a road, alone.

I won't bore you with my escapades during maintenance stand-downs at Long Binh, which took place about every six weeks. The 10-tons would come to wherever the company was and load the D7Es, and take us back, so we had two weeks to make significant repairs to our equipment, see a dentist, get a haircut, get drunk, get laid, go to the steam baths, get new uniforms, and take daily showers. It was common in the field not to wash thoroughly for weeks or cut our hair.

The risks of nightly shelling by the NVA, or Viet Cong, were a constant. We cut off our pants, didn't wear underwear or socks, and just stank and were filthy. The shrapnel tore through our tents and equipment. Sometimes it tore into the bodies of the men; ours, and the mechanized infantry assigned as security for each operation.

5-ton Wrecker

60th LCC NDP Encampment

SP/5 Thomas L. Randle Jr

Most nights, we had a few mortars and RPGs lobbed into our NDP. I often had all 11 tires (10 on the ground plus a spare) and fuel tanks punctured on the wrecker. I would spend an entire day repairing tires and getting the fuel tanks welded to fill the holes; all that before 30 Rome Plows came back to the NDP in the afternoon, where the wrecker would be online to assist. Sometimes the Warrant Officer, a man of Hawaiian descent, whom I called "Pineapple" behind his back, as Mr. Thomas had rotated home after five tours, would yell at me to hurry up.

Temperatures in Vietnam vary. December-March is cool, misty, and cloudy. April-June is warm to hot, with clear skies and sunny. June-August is stormy, hot, and humid. September-November is a mix of sun and clouds, warm to cool. The monsoons affect the Country from October to April. It constantly rains, turning our NDP into a mud bog. Men would occasionally sink up to their armpits walking from the mess truck to their tents, carrying their tray of food; it was sloppy muddy, hot, smelled, and was dangerous. Changing flat tires and welding holes in fuel tanks in all kinds of weather may be under-appreciated.

Pineapple took a chunk of shrapnel in his chest one night. I still see it. He was standing on the tailgate of the parts truck, a deuce and half (2 ½ ton vehicle) when a rocket landed on the dirt in front of him. He said, "Who threw a hammer at me" when he was hit. Then the entirety of his t-shirt turned red. I visited him at the hospital before he was taken to Japan. I gave him a box of cheap cigars because he always had one in his mouth.

At night, the maintenance teams repaired ruptured hydraulic lines and welded belly pans damaged by stumps and land mines on the Rome Plows. Heli arc welding, at night in the jungle, in the open, is not for the faint of heart. An NVA sniper could see that flash for hundreds of yards. We were targets of opportunity. I stayed with the maintenance crews for as long as I was needed. Sometimes I would lay down on my cot, only to be awakened when the wrecker was required to assist.

Towards the end of my 12-month tour, a 750-pound radiator core was dropped on my foot. I had not removed my boot yet, fearing my toes might fall off. It was an accident. We worked too many hours and got complacent. I was lifted by chopper to Long Binh Post. Back in the company area of the 60th, I took a jeep and drove myself up the hill to the hospital. I hobbled into the hospital (*think MASH, like on television*), and saw civilians on stretchers bleeding onto the floor. I turned around and got back in the jeep and finally, that night, removed my boot. It was a mess, but I didn't lose toes.

I did milk the hell out of the injury, as I knew the risks of getting hurt, maimed, or dead only increased if I pushed my luck. I got assigned the job of company postal clerk and wore flip-flops until I got orders to process out of Vietnam. I was a short-timer, meaning I was nearing returning to the States and had had all the fun and adventure a 19-year-old could possibly want.

At that time, a recruiting Sergeant came to see me. He offered to promote me to Staff Sergeant (E6) and approve a $7,500 reenlistment bonus if I committed to 3 more years in this man's Army. I had not yet turned 20, and it was tempting. I had received divorce papers from my teen wife, who had taken up with a sailor. I refused to sign the divorce, mostly because I am hard-headed, stubborn, and angry as hell; and mainly because, by God, I loved my daughter, and I wasn't going to stand for some cowardly sailor having my daughter call him Dad. I stayed mad for another 40 years. I was not diagnosed with PTSD until about age 65.

I then rotated back to the "World" and celebrated my 20th birthday while enroute to Oakland, California.

Afterward, I traveled in civilian clothes as the mood of the Country in 1970 wasn't warm toward returning Vietnam Veterans. I spent a week in Newport Beach with a buddy who was together with me in Germany and Vietnam. I stopped in El Reno, Oklahoma, to see my sister, and got to Jacksonville about two and half weeks after being discharged from the Army in Oakland.

Upon arrival at the Jacksonville airport, I was met by my wife's stepfather and two of his sons. They informed me that my wife had run to hide in Hollywood, Florida, with our daughter, and that they were on my side on the issue. I think my wife had seen too many Rambo movies and thought I was coming home with an M60 machine gun to slaughter her and that sailor. I did think about doing that. But I brought her and the baby back to Jacksonville. We remained married for 16 years in total. We had a son in 1972. She died of cancer about ten years ago.

I remarried in 1985 to the love of my life and enjoyed a life and career as a credit union CEO. My golf game ain't bad. I have published five books and had a consulting practice facilitating leadership training and strategic planning. I am healthy and surrounded by family and friends. I have made peace with God and have spent the past dozen years volunteering in my community and Church.

Vietnam is with me daily. I am on prescriptions from the Veterans Administration for PTSD and was awarded a disability of 70%. I have panic moments and have learned to talk myself down.

While 66% of the men in land clearing teams/units/companies were awarded a Purple Heart, I was not. Lord knows I gave the enemy every chance to put a hole in me. I have learned not to feel ashamed.

I began attending bi-annual reunions around 2008, for all the men who served in any land clearing capacity in Vietnam. We have had as many as 200+ attend. I have reunited with buddies I hadn't seen for over forty years. Our attendance is now thinning, as we are getting older, and many have service-related health issues. Many have died in the past decade of disabilities related to Agent Orange or injuries obtained in Vietnam.

Sharing my story with you is necessary. Soon, all of the Rome Plow operators, guys like me, and the other support soldiers will be dead. Preserving our history is essential. What Rome Plows did in Vietnam had never been attempted before and hasn't been tried since.

SP/4 Keith A. Albert

HHC 86th Engineer Battalion
(Land Clearing Platoon/Team)
1967 – 1968
Equipment Mechanic
Hometown: Florence, South Carolina

Letters From 'Nam

*Keith Albert had grown up within the southern California city
of Whittier, where in 1966 he was drafted into the Army and
sent to South Vietnam the following year. The excerpted content
herein, which was taken directly from letters sent to his parents,
serves to form a condensed version of his writings sent home,
while serving out his tour in Vietnam as an equipment mechanic
with the 86th Engineer Battalion's Land Clearing Team.*

To:
Mr. and Mrs. Mason Albert
14443 Flomar Dr.
Whittier, California 90603

October 12, 1967 (Postcard)
Arrived VietNam 5:00am Oct 12 by their time. Waiting
in Bien Hoa Air Force base for luggage. It's humid here,
not really that hot. Peculiar odor. Good flight.
Hope to get to unit soon. Will write again first chance.
Keith

October 16, 1967

Hello Everyone,

Well here it is Monday, a week later and I'm finally getting around to writing. I started a letter last week' the night they played the last world series game. I couldn't find it the next day so I must have lost it. I was on detail that night and was slightly tired.

Anyway, since I've left the states I've had 3 different addresses. The current one is for the 590th.

159th Engr HHC Const GP

61st Const Support Co

590th Maint Co

All day today I've been on sand bag detail. We were just outside of the compound and had an armed guard. We're stationed about 10 miles from the Bien Hoa airport and out here they really know the war is going on. Any time we leave the compound we carry weapons, ammo, and wear steel pots and flak vests.

While we were on detail today there was a demo team about 150 yards from us blowing up booby traps. It was really interesting.

When I got here yesterday we stood and watched two jets drop napalm not too far away. It was far enough that you couldn't see burn but could hear it explode. Those fool jets look like they drop straight out of the sky and go right straight up. They're beautiful. The compound we're in has quite a few people in it. We've got at least two whole divisions here. One of the divisions is from Thailand. They're a bunch of pretty good jokers. I met some of them down at the E.M. club last night with a couple of other guys from the company. We hooked a ride back with them when it began to rain.

About 5 days ago the V.C. mortared the Thai Division right in the compound. They say it was pretty close to here, about a quarter mile. Last night the big guns in the compound were working for about two hours. They'd fire about every five minutes and shake the whole place.

You wouldn't believe this place. It's the dry season and It's rained at least twice a day. The mosquitoes are bad and would eat you alive if you didn't have a net. I lucked out and got one.

We're lucky enough to have showers here. If they fill the tanks in the morning it's warm by evening. If not, the showers are cold. Someone forgot to fill the tank today and it ran out after only 2 had finished. Some of the guys who didn't get showers were just now outside showering in the rain. A little cold, but it works.

October 25, 1967

I've only got a few extra minutes this morning so will only write a short note.

Everything here is as good as can be expected. It's always hot and even more humid. Even after a shower you start sweating while you dry off. Last night I got caught in the shower when it started raining. It was a bit cold and lasted about 20 minutes.

Right now it's the dry season here and it usually rains about 2-8 inches a day. I can't wait until the rainy season starts.

12:15 AM

It seems I had less time than I thought this morning. I got your letter this afternoon so am also answering that now.

The company here is new in-country and still setting up.

We don't have a shop area as such yet, just a good level field where most of the equipment is. Also, we don't have very much equipment of our own; only a few trucks and jeeps. We aren't authorized any because we're a support unit.

Once we get set up we'll be supporting a Thailand regiment and the 86th Engineers. The Thai regiment is their best infantry. I think they're called Queen's Cobra's

About all I've done since getting here is sandbag. At first I didn't go for the idea but found out it's the next best thing to working at the shop. We get away from the company area and nobody gets mad.

The CO figured each man could fill 75 bags a day. What a laugh. We can do 75 bags per 2 man team in 1 ½ hrs and take a 2 hour break. It seems to work out pretty good. We do the same thing in the afternoon.

October 31, 1967

Well, I'm pretty well settled now in the 590th Maintenance Company, as I've got things well straightened out for what we have to work with. I've said before that this company is new here and we still don't have anything to work with at all.

Also, I'm not doing the work I was trained in. Almost every day I've pulled detail of some kind. They just don't have any equipment here at all, so no work.

Just last week they worked on bulldozers for the 86th Engineers, but I didn't get in on any of that. Tomorrow they're going down by the South China Sea to clear roads. We're sending a contact team along but I'm glad I'm not going.

The area where they're going hasn't been cleared yet

and 2 infantry companies are going along for added protection.

November 11, 1967

As soon as the map gets here I'll try and locate where I
am and let you know. The other guys here say that Long
Binh isn't on the map. I don't know why. It's quite a good
sized place.

No, I still don't have any sun-glasses. I'll round them
up one of these days. Basically I live in a wooden hootch.
It's wooden about 4 feet up then screened in up to the roof.
The roof is a tent like deal and gets pretty warm in the
after-noon. You can see a little of it in the picture I sent.

December 31, 1967

Would you believe I've got radio watch tonight? Ever
since I've been out in the field I haven't had time to do a
thing.

I've been out here since Nov. 17th and time has just
passed. It's good in a way because we're busy all of the
time.

I think I mentioned that some of the people in the company went out TDY with the 86th Engineers' land clearing
platoon. Well, four of us replaced them in November. So,
I'm now living and working with them on a regular basis.

I'll try and give you some idea of where we are. If you
have a map like you sent me it should be all right. First off,
Bearcat is on the map as Bear Cat. It's almost due north of
Bien Hoa. The main highway #1 is shown on the map so
right now we're about 70-80 miles from Saigon.

If you check a small seacoast town called Hon Tam,
we're just below it on Hwy 1. We've been clearing the

jungle on either side of the road for 100 meters and every bridge and intersection for 300 meters. The only engineer equipment we have are Caterpillar bull dozers with angled cutting blades. You may have heard of Rome Plow teams? That's us. There are only 3 in country and this was one of the first ones.

We're out here with the 9th infantry division pulling security for us. We don't pull any guard unless we're on alert nor do we pull K.P. All we really do is work 12-18 hours a day, 7 days a week, as maintennance mechanics, in support of the Rome Plows. We've had a day and a half off since I've been here. We had half a day on Thanksgiving and all of Christmas day.

We've got it pretty good here. It's up in the mountains and there are plenty of streams and small rivers to take a bath in. If we didn't then it'd be 2-3 days between baths. As it stands now, I've had one bath since Christmas.

Tomorrow we're taking the tractors down to a river about 4miles away and washing the debris out of them.

We're only supposed to be here a few more days and then go back to BearCat for about 10 days of straight maintenance and then head back out to the field.

If I come out again I will probably be better prepared. I didn't bring anything I thought to be extra and found I didn't need half of it anyway, and could use a lot of other stuff instead.

Canvas covered wood framed hooch (center of photo) in 86th Engineer Bn LCT area at BearCat

Weapons cache found in Viet Cong Tunnel

Keith Albert, working on new screens for a dozer tree cab

NDP Motor Pool

Some members of the 86th LCT, with large snake

I've received almost all of the packages people have sent. I've been told there is one back at the company that came registered mail. I don't know who sent it or why they haven't sent the mail clerk out here with it but I should find out in about a week.

The two tins of cookies you sent came about 5 days apart, I don't know which one came first but they were pretty well spaced. The box of clothes arrived 2 days before Christmas. I've been saving them until we got back to BearCat so I'll have something to wear.

I also received the box of cheeses yesterday. It didn't last very long because there is no way to keep it once it's opened. I ate quite a bit and we all enjoyed it.

You once asked me if we had any way to heat soups and such. Sure do. Out in the field we eat C rations at noon every day. We use a putty-like plastic explosive material called C-4 to heat the C's with. It works real good when lit, and is completely safe unless compressed suddenly.

Well, can't think of much else to write. I wish I still had all of your letters but it's best to burn them to keep addresses from Charlie.

Keith

January 19, 1968
Hello Again,
Well it's been about 3 weeks since I've written and you're probably wondering where I am.

Right now we're back on the same operation again. We missed a few ARVN camps and we needed to return to cut them. We've been out here 3 days and are going back to BearCat tomorrow.

We had a 10 day stand down or maintenance work

period in BearCat before we came back out. We worked almost around the clock and it seems like a rest to get back out in the field.

We've only got half of the tractors out with us now and when we return to BearCat we're going to pick up the rest and go back out.

All we know about the next operation is that it will last approximately 45 days and will be in the same area where 101st airborne is operating. I think if you check the papers it will probably be the easiest way to find out where I'll be. I'll write again as soon as I have time and let you know what I've found out.

Would you believe I finally made E-4 ? My pay will now go up about $50 every month, so I'm going to send home about $160 a month to the bank.

One nice thing about being out here is there is no place to spend money. I never have been paid for November yet and I've got $200 in the company safe to buy everyone at home something. If I ever get the time, I'll get everything caught up with.

Well, I think I'll close for now and get another letter off tomorrow.

Everything is fine and I'm as happy as can be expected. So much for now.

Keith

February 9, 1968

Well, I received your last letter about 3 days ago and am just getting time to write. I've received 3 from you since I've written but have been working hard.

We're out in the field again but not living in tents at the moment. Right now we're staying at and working out of

155

Bien Hoa air-base. We've been here 4 days now and it's a good kick. We've been in barracks and have use of a club, movie theater, showers and the whole bit.

When we first came out we were in the jungle not far from here. Right after this land clearing effort started we moved to Phu Loi. We cleared some woods where Charlie was hiding and leveled a village he was using as a base camp.

Five of us from maintenance had a ball the day they razed the village. We went thru quite a few houses and took tools and stuff we could use before the dozers buried everything. We also picked up two puppies for mascots and they really helped to pass the time.

We've been working pretty steady so far this operation.

Two nights ago we didn't hit the racks until 2 am, and last night we made it at about 4. Tonight we're off even while there are 13 dead lined tractors.

At any rate things have been petty good lately. The work hasn't been hard and life in general has been pretty good.

Well 'It's about 11 pm, so I think I'll hang it up.

Everything is fine here and pretty good for being in Vietnam.

Keith

February 11, 1968

We worked again tonight until 12:30 am. Because we got almost all of the tractors out we'll get about half a day off tomorrow. We don't have to get up until 10:00 and will be off at 2:00.

We worked late last night also until they had an alert. I've said before that we're in Bien Hoa airbase and it received mortar fire about 12 last night. When the alert was finally over we quit work for the night.

Saigon was supposed to be over-run last night. The ARVN's have a group of V.C. trapped and 4 regiments of V.C. were supposed to take over Saigon and spring them. Just like a jail break.

Up until midnight last night 27,000 Viet Cong had been killed since the beginning of the Lunar new year (Tet). The bad part is that most of them are kids of 15 & 16 years. It seems the V.C. are hard up for recruits. If the war keeps up for very much longer it could be cleared up in a year. It's too bad the military can't run the war like they want to.

I may get a chance to mail a package or two tomorrow. If I get to the P.X. and junk shop, I'll probably have quite a bit of junk to send. I hope I make it.

I don't know if you noticed the return address on the last letter I wrote but I changed it. Since I'll be with the 86th Engineers indefinitely now, it'll be easier to send your mail directly through them.

Sp/4 Keith A. Albert
RA 56690241
HHC 86th Engr BN (CBT) (LCT)
APO SF

February 22, 1968
You won't believe it, but yesterday I was shot in the leg. A little hard to believe, isn't it? But it's true.

I was out on the trace when it happened. The dozers had scared up a small group of wild pigs and we got permission from the mechanized cavalry unit to do some shooting.

One of my friends borrowed a .45 cal. pistol from our medic and we took off after them. We only got about 100 yds when we lost them in a ravine. Before we went back he (my friend) stopped to unload the pistol. When he thought he had it, he pointed the pistol towards the ground and fired it.

Just as he pointed it, I stepped out in front of him and he didn't see me. The bullet caught me on the inside of my right knee. I guess you could say I was lucky because it missed the bone completely.

I suppose if you have to get shot that's the way to do it. A nearly perfect wound.

At any rate I'll be in the hospital for another 2-3 days and then on light duty for a week or two. I don't know how long for sure.

Feb 25, 1968

Well, I've been doing some heavy sleeping the last two days and completely forgot about this letter.

The doctor sewed up my leg yesterday. It took about seven stitches to close it up completely. They opened the wound all the way to clean it out. He said I'll be able to go back to BearCat tomorrow so I'll probably go back to work in about 10 days.

The name of the place we were at was Phu Loi. That's where we picked up a couple of puppies. They're both just mutts but it's fun just playing around with them.

March 2, 1968

Well I've slacked off what I had proposed to do with my writing but it's still better than it was.

Everything has quieted down here for awhile. It seems

just a lot like it was before all the shooting started.

BearCat got mortared three nights ago and we had to hit the bunkers again. A round landed about 150 yds from the building I'm in (86th), and scattered junk all over the roof. I tell you, I was doing some serious moving.

March 12, 1968

The tractors have been working down by Long Binh for about 4 days and will be coming back to Bearcat on Friday or Saturday. Our group is split again and one is up north by Lai Khe. They've only got 8 tractors up there and are just cutting a small section.

One of our operators was hurt up there when a V.C. fired a rocket propelled grenade (RPG) into his cab. He was wearing his flak vest and only received numerous small cuts on both legs, right arm and right side. He's all right now. We went to 24th Evac Hospital yesterday and took him in (smuggled) a couple of beers. That was the only thing he needed when we were there the day before.

My leg is healing up real well now. In 3 or 4 more days the incision they made should be completely closed up. I've only got 3 small spots that are still open. No infection and I haven't been bothered by it in the least. I've been working a little the last few days. Mostly welding where I don't have to put any strain on it or bend too much.

This garrison duty is really getting bad now. It's almost like state side. I'll be glad to get out in the field again and relax with my friends.

The weather has been real nice here. Now it's starting to blow (wind) every afternoon and I expect the monsoon to start within 2 weeks. It sprinkled a few minutes yesterday but not enough to even settle the dust. It's really going to be bad when the mud gets about a foot or two deep. That's when the work will be rough.

The package you sent still hasn't made it, although I'm expecting it any day now. There were a lot of packages held up when the TET offensive started but now they are starting to filter thru. I hope any day for it now.

March 22, 1968

We've been working almost every night since and I've been pretty tired. We're back out in the field again and having a ball.

We're clearing QL-1 between Bien Hoa and Xuan Loc. We were down near Bien Hoa until today when we moved to within 3 miles of Xuan Loc. We've got a total blackout at night here so I'll have time to write letters now.

Everything is going real good now. The only problem we have is new operators who keep tearing something up. We've kept pretty busy, but not so much that we don't get a break once in awhile.

March 30, 1968

Everything is all right here for now. We were expecting some excitement last night. The intelligence had it on good report that there was a battalion sized unit of V.C. headed our way yesterday. This was backed up by sightings of many small groups of them all moving towards us (10-15 men each).

The mechanized Cavalry unit securing us made contact with them late last night. We had an ambush patrol out and they got into a fire fight about a half mile from base camp.

The one thing the Cav doesn't do is back down from

a fight. There are two more Cav units just waiting to come in if we are hit, plus 32 big guns are trained right in, just 100 yards outside of our perimeter defense. If we are hit we're going to clean up on old "Charlie". It should really be a beautiful fight.

September 11, 1968

Well, I do believe you've been waiting and worrying way too long, and I know you believe this too.

Quite a few things have happened over here since I last wrote.

At the present time I'm driving a M548 tracked vehicle. It's an armored cargo carrier but we're using it for a contact truck and it works great. We've got a .50 caliber machine gun on it, mounted on a swivel, and we've had a couple of chances to put it to work. I finally got back on the trace but not in the way I wanted.

Last month just seemed to be a hard one for this outfit. Two of our maintenance people were injured in a land-mine explosion and haven't come back. A kid named Rich Nondorf was disabled for life when he tripped a mine and it took off his right leg, part of one arm and possibly lost an eye. I'm sorry to say that this is the reason I'm back on the trace. I wanted back but not like that.

About 3 weeks later two of our truck drivers were ambushed on the road to BearCat and killed, while hauling a damaged plow back to our motor pool. This operation has taken a heavier toll than at any other time in its history.

We've just come in for another stand-down and will be going back to the IRON TRIANGLE when we leave again. We were up there once for about 2 months and had many nights in the bunkers.

161

We're in Long Binh post now for our stand-down.

I might be getting SP/5 before I leave. CW2 MacCafferty recommended I be promoted before I leave and had also asked to get me a 7 day drop. If I get the drop I'll only have 21 days as of today. No drop means I'll be home around 28 days from now.

Well, I can't think of anything else to say. I'll write again soon if we don't have too much work.

With love,

Your son Keith

SP/5 Paul W. "Dozer Doc" Sanchez

27th Land Clearing Team &
60th Land Clearing Company
1968 – 1969
Equipment Mechanic
Hometown: Hesperia, California

And There I Was Again...

Dave K. was cycled into the 27th/60th as our new welder. Once during our stay, he and I were re-inforcing the plows against land mine blasts. My job then was to hold the thick pieces of one inch steel plate in place while Dave spot-welded the plate first, then heli-arc welded them in, extra strong.

We were working at night, when mortars started to splash in around us. The explosions were buried in mon-soon mud and were pretty much ineffective. The sound was 'bloop bloop' as they detonated, except for the one that landed on the dozer's reinforced cab roof. That one produced a lot of sound and light. Of course Dave missed it while busy welding. But I had noticed, during the mor-tar rain, a M48 battle tank on the perimeter was hit with a Rocket propelled grenade (RPG); and in the morning the 'bent' tank was hauled off by a M88 recovery track vehicle and replaced with another M48A5 combat tank. Dave missed most of the "action" being an intent worker; very mission orientated.

On another day, I was removing the ammunition crates

from the back of my issued M548 tracked cargo carrier. I had been running around the 'cut' with crates of ammo in the form of M79 grenade rounds, M16 5.56mm rifle cartridges, smoke grenades of gray, white, orange, red, green, yellow, and violet, as well as M60 7.62mm and M2 Big Machine Gun (BMG) .50 caliber rounds. There were also fragmentation grenades and pop flares of mixed colors.

Well, this stuff was rattling around on the deck back there, in the cargo bed, until I was tasked with taking a Colonel for a ride back to his chopper. I told him he could ride up front on the long seat to which he chose to ride in back with the crates at his insistence. Later, I decided to off-load and stack the ordinance on the back of a 25-ton "dragon wagon" behind a couple Conex containers of parts and materials.

So then again 'there I was'. I backed up the cargo carrier onto the rear of the trailer and began to push the crates up the incline. I was gathering the boxes at the rear of the bed, jumping down to unload and stack them on the trailer. While, I was standing on the tail end of the cargo deck, I happened to look West, just in time to see a satchel charge fastened to an RPG sail past my head as I jumped down for cover. The thing went off just short of the communication truck. As I was in the air and following the projectile, I saw with my own eyes, the detonation, which produced the largest, darkest black hole that showed it's destructive power. The abyss that it left was surrounded with a brown to orange to yellow halo around the crater's rim. Fortunately, the IED went off at about a four foot depth with the result of the blast blowing mostly upwards, not out. For me that was about the third time I jumped for cover not knowing where I was going to land. As I rolled under the trailer, I was met by a soldier pulling up his pants; himself having scampered away from the latrine to get up under a safer hiding spot. Later, as one situation turned into another, this scenario had occurred when I was following the plows into the cut, and we suddenly entered a VC camp. It was interesting to note among the effects found there, stacks of propaganda pamphlets stating, 'give yourself up to the NVA and they would treat you with respect', with pictures of helmets on rifle butts stuck barrel first into the soil. But of a more serious note, was the still standing whiteboard there. On this board was a Polaroid picture taped to the center with arrows pointing to the transmission-to-engine connection. If an RPG might hit in this area, it would start the magnesium in the case, which would burn until the dozer buckled in the middle from the intense heat. There would be no way to extinguish a fire of that kind with the equipment at hand.

Then suddenly, another "and there I was" moment came as I was helping a dozer restart after running out of fuel. I was bleeding the injectors to start the fueling at the precups (pre-combustion chambers). Half way through there was an attack on our support element. The M113 APC with infantry aboard was backing away from a RGP in flight. I so wanted to shoot at the VC with the Ma deuce .50 caliber on the swivel ring above me on the M548 track, but my mission was to get the Rome plow started and out of harm's way first.

We all had Ripper roster numbers and when the overhead chopper demanded the injured land clearer's name over the radio in the clear, I was perplexed about the request. I checked the dozer for function, even though the command-detonated mine pretty much destroyed the machine's operator as evident by the more than half blood-filled helmet lying on the floorboard. The M548's onboard medic took the wounded soldier to an appointed medivac helo location. I took the dozer, kicking over the helmet when I sat in the seat. Getting back down on the ground, I immediately located the wire that exploded the mine and followed it back to a bunker. I then ripped the top off the position and proceeded to fill the darkness inside with .45 caliber rounds from my M3 submachine gun. When I jumped into the bunker I found several containers of water leaking. Then I discoovered there was a dark tunnel in the side of a dirt wall. I immediately unloaded the rest of the M3's magazine into the black, before taking the D7E tractor back into the cut, to continue taking down the jungle until the medic driven cargo carrier returned with a replacement operator. At that time each section had an officer and a medic aboard each of the three M548 support tracks.

The next great adventure, West of Lai Khe, took the form of watching an infantryman poking a stick at a hornets nest, one of the Winnie the Poo shaped ones. The insects were flooding out of the hole in the bottom when an explosive device went off under a dozer in front of me. The operator who took the blast then appeared on the track, jumping off immediately. In his frantic haste, he had left the vehicle in gear when he exited.

The machine lurched ahead as he jumped clear, and I quickly followed the dozer into the uncut jungle. When we got close to the winch I switched out of the operator's seat of the M548 and stood on the front deck ready to jump aboard the fleeing tractor. I told my replacement driver to bump the tractor's winch housing, at which time I leaped onto it. I then scooted along the outside of the reinforced cab while gripping the heavy screens with my fingers until I managed to make my way inside of it. Jumping into the operator's seat, I stopped the vehicle's forward motion and pivoted in place. As I started to return out of the jungle, the dozer created a path for the maintenance carrier to turn around and follow me out to the edge of the swath. At that time our onboard Lieutenant wanted to know what I was thinking. I got back an important piece of the mission, myself jabbering like an idiot from the hype. Operation West Lai Khe would continue.

In this operation we were established as the fourth vehicle behind three Rome plows going on. I witnessed an operator take a devastating hit from a mine in the minefield which surrounded a VC headquarters that we suddenly found ourselves in. I left the M548 to the medic to operate, as I then sat in the plow's operator seat and put cigarette filters in my ears, fastened my flak jacket, before heading out to cut the jungle. Well, I got about twenty feet when the blade struck another mine. The concussion held dirt, dust and blackness as it halted forward movement. The helmet flew back, flak jacket ripped open and debris filled the air before me. I reset, then went another few feet till the third explosion happened. This time I got out of the cab to inspect the blade for damage. I was met by a staff sergeant, who told me to move away from the minefield. He was in charge of a team of minesweepers, and I was told his people would take it from there. I highly expect that was when my right ear stopped working. I did not know I was affected in a serious way, as everyone yelled to be heard, until I was aboard a C5 Galaxy heading for Japan later that month. The medic aboard the aircraft asked me if I knew I was bleeding. I looked down on the scrub to notice the entire right side was drenched in my blood. He put his watch to my right ear, asking if I could hear it tick. My answer was no, but I could hear the sound in my left ear. Goodbye to stereo music.

Other times:

This narrative would best be served if I started with Tom B. and Joe D Bear asking if they could give me a hand. My reply was something like, "naw I'll get there eventually". My bunk was in base camp. We were to be here two weeks. So, the holiday was free time.

It was the remnant of an afternoon and evening in our base camp at Di An. Having had duty the night before, while running late after a shower, and what was 'supposed to be just a short nap', I got to the mess hall as they were closing up. But the veggie plate was still out, so I picked an olive for Thanksgiving dinner.

Enough of that. My true target that day was the wash, North, at Di An base camp. It's location was to be the next construction site, well within the perimeter and deep as it was long, accommodating over a dozen of us at a time, as our own private open-air gathering spot. When I got to the wash: there standing in the sand, bottles of hard liquor unopen waiting for the ensuing party. Missing was a member of our team who had gone for cigarettes of the 'other' kind.

He did arrive after a bit, however the rest of us by agreement cracked open libations and had imbibed. I unfortunately was a bit overzealous, which turns us to the "moral of the story": Never do that before getting a grip on reality. That said, 'my body was drunk as a skunk, but my mind was as clear as a bright summer day. I later made it to my bunk by sheer force of mind. At times I stumbled, but mostly low crawled until I accomplished the mission at hand.

The next morning I was still drunk on my feet. I was late for formation and my unsteadiness on my feet elicited a roar of laughter from my peers already formed up. The first sergeant then added his stern admonition, while we were then informed to bring our weapons to noon formation. It was odd to have a formation then, much less bring weapons. This first sergeant became the third since I transferred to the 27th Land Clearing team. And as this unit was on 'use them up like match sticks if you have to' type footing with the Army, he encountered a myriad of problems, the least of which was bad manners. He stood out front of the formation, bedraggled, stooped over, kind of like 'broken'. His voice cracking as he proclaimed "you will turn your weapons into the armory", This invoked a response, which to me was somewhat blurry in memory. Shots into the air were fired. At the time the unit was in low numbers, though authorized more than a hundred. Many of those weapons were already loaded, then fired without command. 'Top' then said with voice straining, "You act like wild animals from the jungle!" Whoa, the unified yell of a hundred armed "Jungle Eaters", drunk or sober is a site to behold. I have a suspicion this had to do with the wall that was pushed out of the enlisted men's club by some rowdy soldiers Thanksgiving night.

Stuck in the mud:

As an engineer mechanic, I was often tasked to use a variety of equipment. This operation had me moving down the road in a 10-ton prime mover truck, pulling a

169

25-ton lowbed trailer loaded with miscellaneous heavy Caterpillar dozer parts. When I arrived at the edge of a bog, Dave had already gotten across the deep muddiness there, to safely make it to the other side. As lead plow he's the one to go first; into the cut, minefield, ambush and mire. Fortunately for us he established a winch point on the far side, being the only one across unaided. Everything else wound up getting stuck in the mud over and above the tracks, jeep wheels, and half way up my truck tires which were nearly five foot tall.

I was on the road leading in when I came upon the impediment. My lieutenant met me, and directed me to back up as far as possible. Having done so, the rest of his directive sent me forward, shifting up through the gears until achieving sufficient speed, as I dove off the road having gained enough momentum to drag the trailer clear of the muddy causeway. We spent much of the day getting across a span of only a hundred meters, roughly the length of a football field. This was achieved by attaching winch cables to every heavy vehicle, pulling it to a point where it was transferred to another set of winches being pulled along until transferred again. Comparatively, the infantry support carriers managed to tread through the muck like a duck goes in water.

I spent the next sixty two days sleeping in a hammock. If I thought getting into the Area of Operation (AO) with thirty four Caterpillar Rome plows was hard, getting out with less than a dozen was much more action packed. I gave up my M548 cargo carrier to the rest of the maintenance crew for movement outward and caught a ride in one of the few operational plows. The remaining three fully functional dozers at that time were handicapped by having to tow by way of their winches a broken one behind it. It became common knowledge that our supply of Caterpillars would dwindle to near none at the end of each field operation; this one no different. We followed a path off the raised roadway, until the way narrowed to a deep crevice of a creek and the road. There was a faint scent of tear gas in the air, as if dispensed and dissipated before we got there. As the first dozer drove up onto the road his right track hit a large mine. The next dozer pulled up next to the first and blew his left track apart. At that point, an infantry major hailed me and I stepped out onto the track. He had a modified short barreled M16 slung across his back. And he said, "who's in charge?" to which I looked right then left in an exaggerated fashion and responded with "I guess you are". Next the radio jeep referred to as the 'rat rig' drove up onto the causeway slipping almost immediately to the far side due to the slick muddy conditions. Good thing he did. The next vehicle was my M548 cargo carrier. Clearly no way out except forward, the cargo carrier, which was laden with the remaining crew in the convoy, rolled onto the road. It rumbled up and to the left, moving on about ten feet before it hit a mine and flipped over on its side, spilling soldiers onto the ground in a blast of fire, dark smoke and overpressure. I found out later our maintenance warrant officer was medivac'd out, as he was wounded or busted up by the explosion. It's the way of convoy etiquette that vehicles are not to stop for bent and broken assets other than for immediate care and extraction of the wounded. Picking up the trail belongs to the maintenance sweep team as they are usually equipped with heavy lift and tools. Our turn next, the dozer moved to the road letting the winch play out some slack in the cable fastened to the broken dozer behind. I wasn't in a seat as there is only one big comfortable recliner like chair in the center over the final drives. So, I sat low in front of the fuel tank, leaning heavily into the chair on my left and behind the blast shield (a welded-in placed one inch slab of iron plating). Since I was not the operator, I put my hands over my ears as we crawled onto the path. No way I was closing my eyes. We were waved past the M548 by the Major mentioned before. There, the winch was then engaged and drawn up with less slack to drag the bent dozer behind us. After passing the flipped carrier, off the road we went. The blade set inches over the ground to catch a detonator if there was one, as we barreled toward the distance at two and a half miles an hour, with our destination clearly marked by dust several meters high. About forty minutes later the lowbed driver told us he was darn glad we made it, as we loaded the plow onto the trailer while my chauffeur and I lit upon the ground to get back to safer confines, where we were handed a cold beer and invited to enjoy another.

PTE (Private) David Page

V4 Company, 6RAR/NZ Battalion
(New Zealand Army)
1969 – 1970
Mechanized Infantryman

Through the Eyes of a Kiwi

One operation we were on was giving protective covering to an American land clearing team. Now this was different. It consisted of doing security patrols around the area of operations where they were doing the land clearing. Apparently, these land-clearing operations would last four to six weeks, with various companies having turn about to do the protective coverage.

What were they doing? just that, land clearing? About ten to twelve bulldozers (*D7*), equipped with angled blades about three metres wide, and two metres high, with the inside corner of the blade sharpened like a carving knife, were clearing away the jungle growth for improved security in the area.

There was a nightly maintenance operation where drivers of these machines would carry out blade sharpening with large angle grinders. What with all the manpower, equipment, and accommodation it was like a small village working diligently on the tractors, with all power being supplied by portable generators.

Their daily method of operation was to line up in a staggered but uniform formation, [*like wheat harvesters do in a field of grain*]. They'd just work their way around and around a given piece of bush while cutting and pushing it aside; or if some trees were too big for that, they would just cut away at the trunk with a blade protrusion called a "Stinger" until it fell down. They [*the drivers*] were well protected in their cabs; the blades in front, heavy steel plate under neath, and heavily protected cabs with steel plate and heavy-duty steel mesh screened walls around all sides except the front. Along the top of the blade, they had narrow slits cut out that gave them enough vision control, for seeing their way.

If they came across a [*manned*] bunker system they would radio to the rest of the group, whom each then raised their dozer blades and went into attack mode; turning into the system and keeping on going until it was no more. They would just drive over the top of the bunker and run it down. If the enemy couldn't get out of their bunkers in time, they were just buried alive. Who's going to argue with a bulldozer that's got a curved blade on it two metres high? If the 'dozers' didn't get them; we did. Not very nice? Maybe, but that was war.

The purpose [*or excuse*] for land clearing was to expose the landscape so that the enemy movements could be observed with better application, and it did not give them [*the enemy*] anywhere to hide. In hindsight I think it did a lot more damage than good. There were literally tens of thousands of acres of bush felled and cleared.

This protection game though, was right on for us. In the course of things, we discovered how the American military had looked after its units. For the purpose of this operation, [*which lasted about three weeks*], we were based inside the American base lines, which were quite big, and, open, and it was ok by us.

Anyway, they flew out a mobile kitchen, about the size of a small cargo container, like a street food vendor, only a tad bigger. They manned it with their cooks and with ours. It was a real luxury not having to have field rations for a while. The Americans were amazed at the versatility and imagination of our cooks. They couldn't get over the fact that our cooks could cook up just about anything, so long as ingredients were available.

They even flew out a Post Exchange [PX] shop that was the size of a large shipping container. It sold beer, books, magazines... you name it, and they had it. It stayed there for the duration of the operation. Like I said, the Yanks looked after their own boys.

CPT James A. "Jim" Hier

60th Land Clearing Company (Jungle Eaters)
1970 - 1971
Company Commander
Hometown: Maricopa, Arizona

Welcome to Combat Land Clearing

I was in the 8th Engineer Battalion in Vietnam, 1st Air Cav Division. I had just been promoted to Captain and was serving as the Liaison Officer with the Assistant Division Engineer on the Division Staff. At that time, I was waiting for a company command position with the 8th Engineers to come available. A new Battalion Commander had just taken command when one of the companies became available, and he gave the company to someone else. I was demoralized to say the least. The ADE (my boss), then told me that the 62nd Engineer Battalion was actively looking for a company commander.

Coincidentally, I had been reporting the daily activity of the 62nd; their location and acres cut, to the division commander at the nightly status update meeting for several weeks, but did not actually know what land clearing was all about. I asked my boss if I could go over to Long Binh, in order to talk to the 62nd Engineer Battalion Commander the next day. Being the liaison officer, I had become well-versed in hitch hiking by air all over the area.

The next day I caught a chopper from Phuoc Vinh (1st Cav Headquarters) to Long Binh where the 62nd Engineer

Battalion was based. When I arrived at the battalion head-quarters, I reported to LTC Robert Monfore and told him, "I understand you are looking for me." I told him who I was and that I was looking for a company command. After a short interview/discussion, he said he would take me. I told him that I would need a letter from him in order to get a transfer from the 8th Engineers to the 62nd Engineers. That evening back at the 8th Engineers, I gave the letter of acceptance to the 8th Engineer Battalion Commander. He was shocked but Ok'd the transfer anyway. Two days later, I returned to Long Binh and reported to the 62nd for duty.

While interviewing with LTC Monfore, I met Tom Franz who was also looking for a command position. He wound up getting assigned to the 984th LCC. Tom later wrote "A Day In The Cut", which is an excellent description of daily land clearing operations. (*It is actually one of the stories featured in this book*)

After getting settled in, I was informed that I would be the new CO of the 60th Land Clearing Company. The 60th was just finishing a 45 day cut. LTC Monfore said we would fly out to the cut the next day but 1st LT Young, the acting commander, would finish the cut and bring the company back to Long Binh for a 15 day Maintenance Stand-Down and I would take over then.

The next day, we flew out to the cut and I saw a land clearing operation in action for the first time. As we arrived in the area, it was very evident they had been busy. We flew low over the active cut and the D-9 Rome Plow directly in front of the chopper blew up. We flew through the smoke cloud because we were too close to avoid it. When we circled for a second pass, the crew was already out of the cab and surveying the damage. When we circled around for a third pass, the plow was back in the cut and carrying on like nothing had happened. Welcome to combat land clearing!

When the 60th LCC arrived back in Long Binh for their 15 day maintenance Stand Down and I had taken command, I began to understand the scope of what I had gotten myself into. Thirty D-7E Caterpillar tractors (27 Rome Plows and 3 bullblade dozers), two D-9 Rome Plows, four M548 cargo track type vehicles, a M113 armored personnel carrier command track, a 5 ton wrecker, several 2 1/2 ton trucks, and a Jeep; all of which had to be repaired, overhauled, and rebuilt were now my responsibility. I started learning more about the men in the company. They were 1st Sgt Glenn Layton, Company Clerk Frank Little, Platoon Leaders 1LT James "Spike" Stephenson, 1LT Kevin Rinnard, and 2LT Lee Campbell, along with CWO Joseph Marchese. I also learned that the soldiers had a tendency not to adapt well to civilization (*Long Binh*) and some other military expectations. Their respect for REMFs was also somewhat lacking. All were hard workers but liked to take it easy, tended to drink too much, and fight with others. Some were excellent shoppers/traders/scroungers. Some of the stuff they came up with was really unbelievable. I didn't ask. They wouldn't have told me the truth anyway.

On the last night of the stand down, after all of the plows and other equipment had been loaded to convoy out to the next 45 day cut, we had a Stand Down Party in the maintenance bays of the motor pool.

I don't know who set it up, but it went like clockwork.

1. The mess hall grilled steaks and all the fixings.
2. The band and the girls showed up.
3. The drinking and dining began.
4. The dancing and private tours began.
5. The fights started.
6. The band and the girls left.
7. Party over, around midnight.

At daylight the next morning, we headed out to the jungle for the next 45 day cut.

On my first cut, we convoyed NW of there, up to Song Be, off-loaded the equipment and met up with our security which was a troop from the 11th Armored Cav Regiment. The next day we crossed the Song Be River on a float bridge that had been erected by the 31st Engineer Battalion. Our mission was to open the road and clear both sides from Song Be, north to the II Corps tactical zone boundary. The road had not been used since the French had departed and was completely overgrown. I had done an aerial recon of the route during the stand down and selected a relatively open area about a mile north of Song Be for our first NDP (night defensive position). I sent the experienced Lieutenants with the company to establish the NDP and I would bring up the rear to make sure everyone and everything had made it across the river ok, as I was still learning.

When I finally made it to the proposed NDP site, chaos had arrived and was continuing in full force. All control had been lost. Plows, dozers, security APC's, and Sheridan tanks were running all over the place. One of the APC's had fallen into a ravine and one of the infantrymen on it had been crushed. Since we were only about a mile from Song Be (*1st CAV Brigade Headquarters*), the military police had sent out a team to investigate the accident. My career was over. If there had been anyone there that I could have given my resignation to, I would have done so. I did ask the MP's if I could borrow their helicopter to get an aerial view of the chaos.

When I got into the air, I was amazed. These men of the 60th knew exactly what to do and were doing it. They had cleared most of the jungle out to 500 yards and were pushing up a defensive berm out to about 150 yards, were digging in and berming up fighting positions for the security vehicles, were dozing trenches for the mess, maintenance tents and the command track, and were establishing an LZ (*landing zone*) for helicopter resupply. The ravine that the APC had fallen into turned out to be a deep triangular moat that had surrounded an old French fort. The plow operators had found the only crossing and were busy clearing the overgrown interior.

We had a hot supper that night in our own secured position, and were ready to go for the next 45 days. I decided not to resign after all, but to stick around and see what these amazing engineers would do next. My motto had become: "Tell the men what you want done, give them what they need in order to do it, and get the hell out of the way."

Captain Jim Hier.

About five months later, at the end of my tour in Vietnam, and two 45 day cuts along with three Stand Downs later, the experimental D-9 plow was still going strong, but with a big rippled hump then showing in the cutting blade, left there as a memento of sorts from one of 'Charlie's' land mines.

SSG Roger W. Pond

60th Land Clearing Company (Jungle Eaters)
1971
Equipment Mechanic
Hometown: Carlisle, PA

Snake

My Career in the military started when I was 17. I joined the New Hampshire National Guard and found what I wanted to do in life. In 1962 I was drafted after missing the Guard drills, and was sent to Fort Sill, OK for a tour; then after getting a clearance, I was shipped to Schofield Barracks in Hawaii as a transporter of rockets. As time passed, I re-enlisted and went to Fort Belvoir, VA for schooling in heavy equipment repair of engineer equipment.

After schooling, I was sent to Fort Bragg, NC to an 8-inch self-propelled artillery unit. While there, I applied to the 82nd Airborne and the Green Berets; but before I could transfer, our unit of 8" self-propelled howitzers were sent to Vietnam with the 7/115 Field Artillery. Another 8" artillery unit was moved from Fort Lewis, WA some time before us. So, the outfit didn't rotate as a unit.

They took half of each unit and sent them to the other unit. As a result, I was sent to the 6th battalion, 32nd Field Artillery.

Time was wasted in CONUS for me, as I was a team member of Nukes. I was in Vietnam for 40 months, and at some point, I launched a 2LT off of the gun, and he said "see you in jail." My response to him was "see you in hell."

My punishment for that was to be sent to Germany in mid-Winter, where I went from 70 degrees above to 35 degrees below zero.

I then re-enlisted for 6 years, with the intent of going back to Vietnam; to the very same battalion, but a different battery. We started out from Cam Ranh Bay, moving to the tri-border area of where, geographically, North and South Vietnam and Cambodia all come together. It was where we were eventually used as support for fire bases 5 and 6.

The unit then stood down, due to President Nixon's program of 'Vietnamization', with all of its personnel disbursed to other units, while I was then transferred to the 60th Land Clearing Company, in my secondary MOS as a heavy equipment mechanic.

One day out in the Cut, we had a young guy who, like a magician showcasing one of his tricks, was going to show everyone how to knock down a large standing tree with a bull blade dozer, without benefit of a K/G blade with a stinger on it that the other tractors had, which could otherwise effectively split the trunk and get it to go over more easily. But, on the third attempt when hitting the tree with the standard bull blade up front, the impact caused a large snake to suddenly come crashing down from the upper limbs onto the dozer's hood and quickly ending up inside of the cab with the operator.

Panicking, after putting the gearshift in reverse to urgently move back from the tree, he suddenly decided to abandon the dozer altogether, and immediately jumped off, only to sit on the ground and watch it continue to crawl backwards over the landscape, until a few of the others there quickly jumped into action. To effectively slow it down and get it to stop, a D9 plow was used to go up against it from the rear, as it also ran in reverse, while another man with some balls then managed to climb up and shoot the snake while dis-engaging the transmission.

After that, the guys with the bull blades learned to leave well enough alone and stay away from the standing trees; to just leave them to the tractors with the Rome Plow blades, or to the demolition guys who would simply blast the trunks with the use of C-4 explosives in order to more easily bring them down, while helping to avoid any possibility of equipment operator's errors or their aversions to snakes.

After my time in Vietnam, I went back to Fort Sill, OK to serve as a surveyor; and after almost 13 years serving in the Army, I decided not to re-enlist again, and just quit outright, to give civilian life another try.

So, from there, I simply went back home and got a factory job, and then re-joined the National Guard in Berlin, NH.

But, at some point, most of the factories had closed in the area, and I was again without work. So, my brother, Sergeant Major Pond, who was stationed at Fort Indian Gap, PA, told me to come on down and stay with him, where I could get a job there while re-enlisting again.

While happy to have moved, I had no regrets, even though I was placed in a transportation company that was picked to go to Desert Storm.

But I found that I still loved the Army, so I went wherever I was assigned to go.

I retired a few years later, as a SSG E-6 because I wouldn't be a boot-licking ass kisser to get promoted. So, in 1994

I was out for good, and still have no regrets.
    The military is still special to me.
    Roger Pond, Pastor
    I received the title of Pastor in 2013.

Epilogue

In the aftermath of the Vietnam war, which the North Vietnamese had actually termed as the 'American war', much was brought to bear on both sides of the conflict, as thousands of dead, wounded and maimed participants, together with a similar outcome for many innocent South Vietnamese bystanders, had borne the brunt of it all while feeling the full force of its fury upon them. The wounded and maimed, while they had survived, many were left with unexpected disabilities that were exceedingly hard to deal with, whether physically or emotionally.

But despite these harsh realities of war, the survivors on both sides were left with the added reality of having to repair their own lives while trying to move past the ugliness of life as it was. For the American Soldier, Sailor, Marine, or Airman, upon returning to the states, many of them found that the life they enjoyed prior to going to Vietnam could never really be the same for them again; not in the sense of how it was before, anyway. For the former Viet Cong and North Vietnamese soldiers, it can only be surmised that they also had a hard time dealing with the war's aftermath, as they had suffered much while losing many more thousands of their own men in comparison, even though they were told by their government that they had won the war and have good reason to rejoice.

However, this sort of thing wasn't entirely new to men and women returning from a war zone after serving in combat. It is safe to say that many of the various personnel who had returned from all of Earth's past wars had exhibited some of the debilitating signs of the very same phantom malady that we now have a name for, in the form of PTSD, which stands for Post Traumatic Stress Disorder. The name now serves as a more accurate identifier for a psychological condition that previously had a few other inappropriate handles to suggest what it was. During both of the American involved World wars and the Korean war, the term, 'Shell Shocked' was commonly used to describe what a soldier was going through, along with, 'Combat Fatigue' and 'War Neurosis'. Although, those previous terms had never really helped all that much in gaining more understanding of the condition. In some cases, ignorance had also come into play during war time, as some in higher positions of the military, especially during the time of the American Civil War and the two World Wars, had inappropriately and unfairly branded those who had exhibited signs of this condition as being 'weak' and 'cowardly'.

For some, whose experiences in the Vietnam war were overly stressful from combat situations, their levels of exhibited PTSD were seen as being considerably higher and less manageable. They had experienced episodes of extreme fear and trauma which affected them to no end, as a result of their own encounters with the enemy and the concentrated mental after-effects that came as a result of what they went through. However, most returning servicemen had somehow learned to deal with their form of psychosis for the most part, in different ways, to effectively help with the day to day management of it, while moving forward with their lives; even while knowing that it was still there, lurking in the shadows of one's own psyche, with occasional flashbacks and panic attacks occurring from time to time, seemingly without any rhyme or reason.

But the good news is that the Veteran's Administration now recognizes PTSD as a somewhat treatable condition, while they have included it among the other service-connected disabilities that they provide compensation for, along with sessions of psychiatric therapy and the observation exercise of meditation. But even still, there are some surviving veterans of the Vietnam war who continue to find it hard to function with this condition, even after 50+ years removed from those bygone days. In some cases, the spouse of the affected former service member has also been known to suffer to a certain extent, through the ramifications of this trauma induced mental illness, as its debilitating effects often leave the couple's social life and well-being in a constant state of dysfunction.

When locating numerous former land clearing engineers over the years since just before the Millennium, I spoke on the phone with a woman whose husband had a severe case of PTSD. While he refused to speak with me, in fear of stirring up old memories, she stated that she had longed to be able to go out socially again, or to travel, even if only once every now and then, while painfully resigned to the fact that her husband's fears and emotional instability had altered their lives in such a way to render them both as social invalids. Needless to say, they would not be attending any land clearer's reunion that I was promoting.

However, despite that unfortunate disabling aspect of PTSD, many other service members had returned from Vietnam, detemined to forget their negative experiences while getting on with their lives. Somehow, they had made peace with things, and were quite able to become active and productive members of their communities across

America, while maintaining a happy home life and raising children in as normal a fashion as could be expected.

But, as this relates to most of the former land clearers who had served in South Vietnam and had later attended reunions, many felt that what they did and what they accomplished was very important to note, while some were even eager to talk about their various experiences in the jungle, despite whatever degree of PTSD they may have carried around with them throughout all these years since. Their shared stories had brought further meaning to others who also served within those elite engineer units, while having performed the same tasks by pitting themselves and their Rome Plow tractors up against the targeted areas of jungle and the enemy who resided within. So many of these men, including myself, had been haunted over the years since working as land clearers, with this unusual yet vitally important involvement having left an indelible mark to one degree or another, on all of our individual psyches.

In having put together this book of shared stories, it is my hope that what was given here by these former land clearers may serve in a broader sense as a reminder of what was sacrificed and what was achieved through the use of the Rome Plow tractor. When addressing the seemingly insurmountable problem of out-of-control enemy insurgency that land clearing operations had faced, it was found that the men of the various land clearing units were not only able to deal with this problem head-on, but were actually able to champion it.

While the U.S. involvement at the war's end had turned out to be an unsuccessful effort within the country of South Vietnam for a variety of reasons, most of which were political, it was clear that our military did not actually lose the war. But it was also clear to many, including myself, that the land clearers' efforts in South Vietnam, through sweat and blood and grit had done just what the Army Corps of Engineer's *great experiment* was designed to do. Through their unselfish actions and amazing resourcefulness, these various units of courageous combat engineers had accomplished and achieved the overall goal according to the plan, despite the war's outcome, and despite the tragic loss of valiant participants along the way, in what had previously seemed to be an impossible task; thereby ensuring that Land Clearing operations in South Vietnam, from concept to full fruition, would ultimately become a complete success.

About the Author

Having grown up in the small San Ramon Valley town of Alamo, California – Located in the San Francisco east bay area, it was a much simpler time for a curious youngster back then, when everything moved at a considerably slower pace; where everyone pretty much knew everyone else in the sparsely populated community, and where most home telephones, while set up on a neighborhood party line, were still operated with a crank type ringer with which to call on the local operator to help make the connection for a local or long distance call. Anything new was generally something to behold at that time, like when the Soviet Russian satellite 'Sputnik' was seen streaming overhead in the night sky against billions of bright stars and distant galaxies in the background, as a strange steady dot of light that moved along in the upper atmosphere, like nothing seen before.

Television was also something quite new back then, during the post world war II Eisenhower years; and my family of nine (*two parents and seven kids*) was one of the first in my neighborhood to get one, as my father was able to afford it, given that he was the elected Sheriff of Contra Costa County at the time. Prior to that, all of our news and information, along with entertainment depended mostly on one's imagination for visualization, while listening to what had regularly been broadcast over the radio. It was a time when the country was transitioning from the somewhat uncertain culture of the Depression-era 1930's and 40's, into a new awakening of war-free life, with high hopes for a new wave of things to come. For myself, growing up during that interesting time period seemed quite ideal, as life was easy in most respects back then for a young boy with much to learn and much to discover about the world around me. But as the 1950's advanced into the 1960's, I found myself moving from grammar school to high school, as the innocence of childhood faded with the passing years, while watching the assasination of JFK on our console encased black & white television, along with the spectacle of the first astronauts to land and walk on the Moon. Then after my senior year of high school, while seeing reports on the war in Vietnam, and hearing about some who had been drafted to serve over there, I then found myself at the age of conscription while dreading the very thought of getting drafted and being forced to serve as a "grunt" infantryman where I might be more apt to step on a landmine and lose my legs, if not my life.

So, with careful thought, I decided to enlist in the Army during the Fall of 1967, to get into a school that would teach me a skill that would likely keep me from that previously mentioned scenario. With that decision, I had put all of my faith into the alternate prospect of becoming a heavy equipment operator. So, I signed up and took basic training at Fort Lewis, Washington, just outside of Tacoma, near Seattle, and was then sent to Fort Leonard Wood in southern Missouri, after 8 weeks of being humiliated and forced to conform to the strict and traditional ways of the United States Army.

At Fort Leonard Wood, I was assigned to a training company that studied and trained on different types of heavy equipment in a somewhat remote area on base called "The Million Dollar Hole". The training course ran from late Fall and early Winter at that time, and it was an exceptionally cold period there in which to train in, with a layering of snow and ice covering portions of the red clay lanscape, and freezing wind making for an even colder situation, as we worked the equipment and alternately tried to keep warm with the use of wood fires burning inside of several 55-gallon steel drums. Whenever I wrote to my folks back home in sunny California at that time, I usually marked the return address on the envelope as 'Fort Leonard Wood, Misery.'

Because my job placement (MOS) had called for me to be trained as a heavy bulldozer operator (62E20), I became familiar with the dozers they had on hand, while initially becoming familiar with a Caterpillar D7S, which was an older and somewhat unusual tractor from the 1930's and 40's, given that its main diesel powered engine had to be started by utilizing a side mounted gasoline powered 'Pony engine' as an assist. It had a manual stick shift transmission, and the blade was operated and controlled by way of cables and pullies. This was the dozer that helped to carve out many areas north of Seattle and Vancouver, BC back in the 1940's, in shaping and filling the landscape for the construction of the famous Alaskan-Canadian or ALCAN Highway, which winds north over rough landscape and through remote areas from Vancouver, British Columbia, through the Yukon Territory, and all the way up to Fairbanks, Alaska.

During the training period, I also became familiar with two of the newer tractors of the day, in the form of the Allis Chalmers HD-16, and the Caterpillar D7E, which were both turbo diesel powered, with 3-speed automatic shift transmissions, and both were fully hydraulic, with regard to the operation of the blade and the rear Hyster winch.

After that secondary training, I received a certificate of completion and flew back home on a 30-day leave, before having to report in at the Oakland Army Base to process through and get aboard a World Airways Boeing 707 flight to South Vietnam, where I spent the next 18-months of my 3-year enlistment involved with the arduous task of leveling and reshaping parts of the landscape there.

Other than that brief history of my early schooling and military involvement during my stretch in the Army, my later enthusiasm and overall prowess for writing, while having ultimately become an author in 2007 with my first book about land clearing, titled 'Clearing Vietnam,' was largely a self-taught adventure, where constant curiousity helped to propel my further understanding of words and their meaning and correct useage, along with how to properly construct and convey what you really want to say in print.

Essentially, it was a reconstruction project that was ongoing inside of my mind, where I was at least able to use what I had learned in my high school English class to help guide me toward what I like to refer to as 'Word Farming'. Call it 'corny', if you will, but short of being noted as a writer or an author, I thought metaphorically that I might actually prefer to see myself as a word farmer who sets the subject seed in my own cultivated mind while fertilizing it with memories and knowledge and a good measure of diction, before watching the words and sentences form and grow to the point of fruition, and ultimately to a time of harvest.

With this in mind, a silly thought had envisioned me standing in Grant Wood's famous 1930 'American Gothic' painting, wearing bib overalls and a red bow tie, while holding a very large upright pencil.

ABOOKS

ALIVE Book Publishing
is an imprint of Advanced Publishing LLC,
3200 A Danville Blvd., Suite 204, Alamo, California 94507

Telephone: 925.837.7303
alivebookpublishing.com